BUYING INTO FAIR TRADE

Buying into Fair Trade

Culture, Morality, and Consumption

Keith R. Brown

NEW YORK UNIVERSITY PRESS

New York and London

NEW YORK UNIVERSITY PRESS
New York and London
www.nyupress.org

References to Internet Websites (URLs) were accurate at the time of writing.
Neither the author nor New York University Press is responsible for URLs
that may have expired or changed since the manuscript was prepared.

Library of Congress Cataloging-in-Publication Data
Brown, Keith R.
Buying into fair trade : culture, morality, and consumption / Keith R. Brown.
pages cm
Includes bibliographical references and index.
ISBN 978-0-8147-2536-8 (cl : alk. paper) — ISBN 978-0-8147-2537-5 (pb   ) —
ISBN 978-0-8147-2538-2 (e-book) — ISBN 978-0-8147-2539-9 (e-book)
1. Consumption (Economics)—Moral and ethical aspects. 2. Consumption
(Economics)—Social aspects. 3. International trade—Moral and ethical aspects.
4. Social responsibility of business.   I. Title.
HB835.B76 2013
306.3—dc23   2012043772

New York University Press books

Manufactured in the United States of America

c   10 9 8 7 6 5 4 3 2 1
p   10 9 8 7 6 5 4 3 2 1

CONTENTS

ACKNOWLEDGMENTS

All authors are asked why they chose to write about their selected topic. I tell my colleagues that I chose to write about fair trade because I wanted a case study to explore culture, morality, and markets. This answer seems to satisfy them, but it is really a bit of a lie. I chose to study the fair-trade movement because of a series of meaningful moments throughout my life. When I was young, my mom worked for Bell Atlantic and had to both sell products to customers and listen to their many complaints. I remember her telling me some of the strategies she had to use to defuse their anger. My dad often worked at home selling supplies for a fire safety company. I remember listening to him tell jokes and talk politely in a loud voice over the phone. I also remember him hanging up, cursing, and screaming after many of these same calls. I distinctly remember my excitement playing a stock market game in the sixth grade where we were taught to make "educated gambles" about which stocks would become profitable. (The team that won took the riskiest strategy by putting all its money on one stock.) In college, I remember the C that I "earned" in my undergraduate microeconomics course. Although I had a great professor, I could not accept all the assumptions in economics about rational consumer behavior. I ended the course by writing a mediocre paper on Max Weber's *The Protestant Ethic and the Spirit of Capitalism* and then switched my major to sociology. After college, I accepted a job as a financial planner. I quit after my first day, in part because I didn't want to wear a suit and because my boss said that I would have to change my haircut in order to attract more customers.

In all these instances, shared meanings (or culture) profoundly shaped economic decisions. My mom was trained to talk in a soothing voice to her irate customers, my dad hid his backstage personality from his customers while trying to make a sale, the shared understandings about mergers helped a sixth-grade team win the stock market game (they invested heavily in Kraft), and a required haircut may have shaped my career trajectory. As for the economics course—well, at the time, introductory economics courses talked little about nonrational behavior. Times have changed, and many behavioral economists are looking at how culture, ethnicity, and identity influence markets. In recent years, sociologists, psychologists, and marketers have also adjusted their theoretical lenses and focused on the importance of culture and morality in markets. This is the area that has always interested me, and it is the focus of *Buying into Fair Trade.*

I would first like to thank the members of the fair-trade movement who welcomed me into their homes, allowed me to attend their meetings, agreed to participate in one- and two-hour interviews for just a cup of coffee, let me volunteer in retail stores and off-site fairs, and provided me with inside access to a world I knew very little about. The great majority of people that I approached for interviews agreed to sit down and speak with me. Members of Ten Thousand Villages agreed to let me observe their stores and even provided insight into their marketing strategies. Members of the Independents Coffee Cooperative let me follow them around like a groupie. I attended their meetings, followed them to fair-trade events, and listened to them talk about the merits of fair trade to college students, business leaders, and customers. A number of individuals are particularly worth thanking for introducing me to others in the movement and for encouraging me to complete this project: Doug Dirks, Joe Cesa, Jacqueline DeCarlo, and Jill Fink. I continue to be inspired by the work they and countless others do within the fair-trade movement.

My colleagues at the University of Pennsylvania greatly shaped this project. Robin Leidner has provided more support than I could have expected. She offered extensive comments on every draft that I sent to her and guided me throughout this project. David Grazian listened and critiqued countless half-baked ideas. He always helped me focus on the big picture. Randy Collins amazed me with the speed at which he was able to provide feedback on early drafts. I am incredibly grateful for the time he devoted to this project. And Bill Bielby provided smart, insightful feedback on the versions that I sent to him. I thank them all for their thoughtful and critical insights.

At the University of Pennsylvania, I was fortunate to have found a network of friends and scholars who read many early drafts of this book: Silke Roth, Adair Crosley, Jamie Fader, Stefan Kluseman, Jacob Avery, Chuck Bosk, and Simone Polillo. I was incredibly lucky to share similar research interests with Frederick Wherry. Fred's constant prodding to "just write it," along with his insights into economic sociology, greatly aided this book. The sociology department provided summer funding through the Gertrude and Otto Pollack Summer Research Fellowship, which allowed me to travel to Nicaragua. Although I feel as if I have been working on this project for a lifetime, this book would still be "in progress" if not for the ethnographic training, financial support, and gracious colleagues that I found at the University of Pennsylvania.

Many others spent time reading chapters of this book. Bryant Simon spent countless hours reviewing the manuscript at both early and late stages of development. Bryant was always able to see through my murky ideas and point me in a clear direction. Debbie Becher, Patricia Tevington, and Susan Clampet-Lundquist also read drafts of these chapters and provided very helpful feedback. Maria Kefalas helped me rethink and rewrite much of chapters 1 and 3. I found moral support and mostly maintained my sanity through working alongside great friends such as Meredith Rosner, Cathy Van de Ruit, Lijun Yang, Carolanne Saunders, Allesandro Pratesi, Evelyn Patterson, Faye Glass, Phil Anglewitz, and Rachelle Brunnn.

Although I worked on this book at the University of Pennsylvania, the seeds for many of the ideas in it were planted at the University of Massachusetts–Amherst. I benefited greatly from the ideas of colleagues and mentors such as Joya Misra, Rick Fantasia, Sarah Babb, Agustin Lao-Montes, Jonathan Woodring, Suzanne Model, and Brian Kapitulik. Joshua Carreiro read many of the chapters in this book and provided much-needed critical insight.

Many others gave their time and effort to this book. Cindy Blohm and Amy Van Stauss read numerous drafts and greatly aided in the copyediting of the manuscript. My sister, Pamela Lowe, took most of the pictures that appear in the book. Laura Wall Starke generously sent me her transcriptions of Paul Rice's talk at a fair-trade conference in Philadelphia. My parents spent many hours watching their grandchildren while questioning what I was doing at work when I wasn't teaching. I hope this book will prove to them that I was "doing something."

I presented drafts of this book at various conferences, where I received feedback from experts in consumer culture, the sociology of culture, and economic sociology. The feedback from Juliet Schor, Craig Thompson, Andrew Perrin, Daniel Cook, Michael Burawoy, David Gibson, Robin Wagner-Pacifici, and Jeff Coburn helped me think deeper about many of the ideas in this book. Often, it took me many months to appreciate the depth of their comments.

I finished this book while working as an assistant professor at Saint Joseph's University. I could not have asked for more supportive colleagues than I found at Saint Joseph's. I have been able to teach classes on fair trade and ethical consumption. In a number of instances, my interactions with students in the classroom helped me rethink my ideas. I have also received summer research funding fom Saint Joseph's University, which helped me devote more time to writing. Alicia Wolf-Lewis provided invaluable research support while I was writing my book proposal. Jessica Wallace devoted more time to this project than I ever could have imagined; she read each chapter twice and provided invaluable research support.

I feel very fortunate to have this book published by New York University Press. Ilene Kalish helped me throughout this project and patiently guided the book along. Aiden Amos and Alexia Traganas have also provided helpful support. Three anonymous reviewers were particularly helpful in shaping this book. The final version of this book is much improved because of the extensive hours they spent reviewing this manuscript.

This book would not have been possible without the support of mentors and professors who shaped my academic career. Most important, Tim Clydesdale's research methods class inspired me to become a sociologist. It was one of the hardest and most rewarding classes that I took at The College of New Jersey. Tim spent an inordinate amount of time revising my papers, and I am certain that I would not have become a sociologist if I had not taken his classes. To him, I am incredibly grateful.

Conducting an ethnographic project is incredibly time consuming. I missed many important events because of travel and commitments to this project, and I thank my family and friends for their patience. I am particularly indebted to my partner, Kathleen Brown, for helping me finish this book. She read and commented upon multiple drafts of every chapter. Kathleen and I have begun to raise two beautiful girls since I began this project. I dedicate this book to both Ella and Alyssa.

1

A Taste of Life in the Nicaraguan *Campo*

During my first night in the *campo* (countryside), I was alert to un-familiar sounds: a bat flew in and out of my room, roosters crowed throughout the night, and a woman pounded fresh corn tortillas before the sun rose. My room looked like it had been used for storage before being converted into lodging for fair-trade ecotourists. It was damp because of the dirt floor and the incessant rain. The wooden walls were dilapidated and almost transparent. Unlike our host families, who had no such protections, my fellow travelers and I slept under nets to pro-tect us from mosquitoes carrying malaria and dengue fever.

I later learned that the rest of our group was also experiencing culture shock. Stacey and Alyssa woke to the sound of a pig being slaughtered; Mike was surprised to see young children carrying machetes to work the coffee fields; and Christopher, somewhat arrogantly, I thought, ex-pressed frustration at the unsanitary way food was being prepared, ask-ing, "How much does bleach really cost?" Why, I wondered, had these fair-trade activists paid more than $1,200 for the chance to stay here?

For ten days, I lived alongside fourteen travelers who wanted to learn more about Nicaragua and fair-trade coffee. Although there is not total agreement over the definition of "fair trade," most supporters agree that fair trade is a "social movement," not simply a "brand." The most holistic definition of fair trade is endorsed by Fairtrade Labeling Organizations International (often called Fairtrade International or FLO), the World Fair Trade Organization, the Network of World Shops, and the European Fair Trade Association, all of which are prominent fair-trade organizations:

> Fair trade is a trading partnership, based on dialogue, transparency, and respect, that seeks greater equity in international trade. It contributes to sustainable development by offering better trading conditions to, and securing the rights of, marginalized producers and workers—especially in the South. Fair Trade Organizations (backed by consumers) are actively engaged in supporting producers, in awareness raising and in campaigning for changes in the rules and practices of international trade.[1]

We all signed up for this trip after hearing that Global Exchange hosts learning tours, or what it calls "reality tours," to communities where fair-trade coffee is grown. (Global Exchange describes itself as "a human rights organization dedicated to promoting social, economic and environmental justice around the world.")[2] Five of the travelers were juniors and seniors from a progressive high school in Vermont. Their parents had sent them to live in Nicaragua for four weeks so that they could learn about the political economy of the region. Everyone on the trip knew about fair trade, but a few had signed up primarily so that they could experience life in a Spanish-speaking country. Our ages ranged from sixteen to sixty-four. Two participants were especially strong fair-trade advocates, most seemed to be aligned with left-leaning political groups, and everyone had previously traveled outside the United States. We arrived in Managua, the capital of Nicaragua, in late December 2005 and traveled by bus to coffee-growing communities north of Matagalpa.

We lived in groups of twos and threes in the homes of the farmers. Each morning, we awoke at 6 a.m. My hosts, Bernabe and Maximina, whom everyone in the community referred to with the honorific titles "don" and "doña," woke much earlier to prepare for the day ahead. On our first morning, we joined don Bernabe, his grandson, and his grandson's friend to pick coffee in their nearby fields. We stopped along the way to eat carrots out of the ground, oranges from the trees, and some exotic fruits I had never seen before. It was a cool, quiet morning punctuated by the howls of monkeys sitting in the trees where we picked coffee cherries. (At this point in their growth, the beans are encased in a bitter-tasting pulp called a cherry.) After a few minutes of picking, I noticed two young girls staring at me and at my fellow *gringo* traveler, Christopher. They were don Bernabe's granddaughters. One of the girls wore what I immediately assumed to be a donated pink dress that looked like it had been worn by a little ballerina; the other girl did not have any shoes. I guessed that their ages were about four and six but later learned that they were each three years older. They were in the fields to help us work but spent an equal amount of time playing. The two girls and don Bernabe's other grandchildren ended up shadowing us throughout our visit. We picked coffee together, played baseball in the dense jungle, and competed in card games of Go Fish at night.

Our group's itinerary, put together by Global Exchange, kept us busy: we met with union activists, toured a coffee plantation to see how it contrasts with a fair-trade cooperative, heard all about the "coffee crisis," learned how coffee gets from the tree to our cups, and were inundated with stories about the benefits of fair trade. We were overwhelmed with facts, but, for me, the face-to-face interactions with fair-trade coffee farmers had a greater impact on how I viewed this system of trade. Playing with the young children, eating with our host families, and sharing stories with coffee farmers all were memorable experiences and fostered a growing allegiance to fair trade.

By the end of the ten-day trip, I was physically exhausted and emotionally drained. I had never before seen levels of poverty like those in both the towns and the countryside of Nicaragua. In Matagalpa, a bustling town in the mountainous northern region of the country, we saw countless children begging in the street when they could have been in school. In the *campo*, we saw malnourished children and met with parents working tirelessly to keep their kids healthy. In both locations, we saw starving stray dogs that acted as a haunting reminder of the ever-present poverty.

I feared I would not be able to explain to my family and friends what I had seen. On the flight home, I was thinking about these issues when the young woman sitting next to me, Harriet, told another passenger that she was working at an international nongovernmental organization (NGO) located in northern Nicaragua. She had not traveled with our group, and I was surprised to learn that she had extensive knowledge of coffee production and fair trade. I struck up a conversation and asked Harriet how she was able to explain to others how fair-trade benefits coffee farmers.

Harriet said she had moved to Nicaragua in 2002 after finishing college. Around the same time, the price of coffee plummeted to forty-one cents a pound, a one-hundred-year low.[3] The price did not consistently return to more than a dollar a pound until late 2006.[4] This coffee crisis devastated farmers around the world. In Central America, plantation owners stopped paying their coffee pickers because it was costing more to grow the coffee than owners could earn by selling it. Malnutrition, already a problem, reached epidemic proportions. Young children could not get enough to eat, and hundreds of thousands of people migrated to cities, where they were often unable to find work.[5]

Harriet was living with a family that grew coffee when the youngest son became gravely ill. He was malnourished, and the family did not have access to health care. Seeing this six-year-old boy die greatly affected Harriet, but nothing had prepared her for the reaction of the boy's older brother, who "jokingly" said, "At least this means there will be more food for the rest of us."

Upon returning home, the activists from my trip told similar, though often less dramatic stories about poverty, life in the *campo*, and the impact of fair trade. They viewed the trip as a success because they had gotten a firsthand glimpse of how fair trade benefits farmers. As an ethnographer who is trained to systematically study culture, I had a harder time processing what I had seen. I kept asking myself, "What kind of researcher studies a place for only ten days and comes to any meaningful conclusions?" So, about a month after I left Nicaragua, I began to contact my fellow travelers to ask about the trip's effect on them. I learned that many had written letters to their local newspapers. Others had petitioned their local supermarkets to carry fair-trade coffee. And still others had given PowerPoint presentations to their coworkers, churches, and elementary schools about the benefits of buying fair-trade-certified products. Even the traveler who had been most skeptical about fair trade became a strong supporter.

I began to understand that my initial search for objectivity had been foolish. Instead of trying to determine how beneficial fair trade is for coffee farmers, I needed to turn my attention to how activists construct meaning during reality tours to places like Nicaragua. I began to understand how these trips transform travelers and encourage them to "buy more fair-trade" products when they return home. Just like the overly dramatic description of traveling to Nicaragua in my introduction to this chapter, fellow fair-trade travelers returned home with powerful stories about the poor living conditions of farmers and artisans. They often tell stories that sound exotic because they do not understand much about the political and economic histories of the places they visited. But even if they are knowledgeable, as I explain in chapters 3 and 5, travelers often exoticize the poor living conditions of far-off producers to convince others of the merits of fair trade. As my project expanded, I met with consumer activists, fair-trade store owners, and NGO employees who are active in the fair-trade world. These individuals all told me that meeting face-to-face with fair-trade artisans and coffee farmers had greatly altered their understanding of fair trade. Instead of reciting facts about the benefits of fair trade, most of them focused on a memorable experience meeting a fair-trade farmer or artisan. These encounters had convinced them that they had seen for themselves how their actions as shoppers can make a difference in the world.[6]

Buying into Fair Trade takes an in-depth look at the fair-trade market. It is a book about how American consumers who identify as socially conscious think about altruism within an increasingly global economy. It explains how consumers navigate the moral hazards involved in trying to shop ethically when so many products are produced according to standards that do not align with their ideals. *Buying into Fair Trade* explores the social forces, from record high oil prices to growing awareness of global warming to declining trust of the government, that lead consumers to shop ethically. It examines the latent rules involved in the search for status as an altruistic consumer and describes the microdynamics of face-to-face interactions that impact our everyday search for moral purity through shopping. In showing how consumers first learn about, understand, and sometimes ignore the ethical implications of shopping, this book sheds light on the potential for the fair-trade market to reshape the world into a more socially just place. Before examining these issues, however, we need to understand the origins of fair trade and how this movement is constantly in tension with market norms.

Fair Trade: Market and Movement Tensions

The origins of fair trade are diverse, and it is difficult to pinpoint one person, event, or even place where the current fair-trade movement originated. I focus primarily on two mission-driven organizations that helped grow the fair-trade movement in the United States. Whereas many companies that sell fair-trade products enter this market to increase profits, both Ten Thousand Villages and Equal Exchange have sought to keep the improvement of the lives of their suppliers at the forefront of their goals. Before describing the growth of these pioneers of the handicraft and coffee markets, it is worth pointing to one significant social change that facilitated the growth of these markets.

In the middle of the twentieth century, cheaper and more efficient telecommunications and transportation systems greatly altered the ways individuals interact with each other and view themselves within the world. These trends, often referred to as defining aspects of globalization, exposed many individuals to wider ranges of cultures, peoples, and experiences. Critics note that globalization has fostered greater economic inequalities within the global "world system." For instance, the sociologist Anthony Giddens writes, "the share of the poorest fifth of the world's population in global income has dropped, from 2.3 percent to 1.4 percent between 1989 and 1998. The proportion taken by the richest fifth, on the other hand, has risen."[7] But globalization has also heightened awareness about the ill effects of global inequalities.[8] Today, it is clear that an increasing number of consumers are looking critically at the social, cultural, and economic ramifications of their everyday purchases.[9]

Products certified as fair trade are sold in order to improve the social, economic, and environmental living conditions of producers in Central and South America, Africa, and parts of Asia.[10] In 1946, Edna Ruth

Byler, a member of the Mennonite Church, began importing embroidered pieces from impoverished women in Puerto Rico. Byler's primary goal was to improve the living conditions of these women. She correctly believed that selling attractive hand-sewn embroidery was a sustainable means for doing so. Sales of these products, as well as her later imports from Palestine and Haiti, continued to increase, and Byler's growing mission-driven business was later acquired by the Mennonite Church and renamed SELFHELP Crafts.[11]

Today, that same business is called Ten Thousand Villages and is one of the largest not-for-profit fair-trade organizations in North America. The current name was inspired by a quotation from Mahatma Gandhi: "India is not to be found in its few cities but in the 700,000 villages. . . . [We] have hardly ever paused to inquire if these folks get sufficient [income] to eat and clothe themselves with." The goal of Ten Thousand Villages has been to provide "fair" income to artisans in developing countries by telling their stories and by opening up a market where they can trade their handicrafts.[12]

Ten Thousand Villages was founded around the same time that Alternative Trade Organizations (ATOs) began to open throughout Europe. These shops originated in the mid-1900s and expanded more rapidly in the 1960s and 1970s. These ATOs created networks of "world shops" in cities throughout Europe to sell handicrafts. These stores were all associated with developmental initiatives in impoverished regions and often had close ties with churches and other charitable organizations.[13]

Like that of the ATOs in Europe, Ten Thousand Villages' rise has been slow and steady. The organization relies heavily on volunteer labor within its retail stores. This keeps its costs low and allows it to return more profits to artisans. Volunteer labor has its drawbacks (high turnover, problems with reliability), but it also ensures that the volunteers support the goals of the organization. Having a deep commitment to the values of an organization encourages staff to work harder than staff who do not share these values.[14]

Ten Thousand Villages also grew because of the rise of identity marketing. Consumers who purchase its products are buying much more than handicrafts and coffee. They are buying the stories behind the products, stories that align with the type of person the consumer aspires to become.[15] Americans took twice as many trips overseas in 2009 as they did in 1988.[16] As they travel more, they look for ways to tell stories about their trips, they look to support impoverished groups they met along the way, and they look for products that reflect their own ethnic heritage. The products sold at Ten Thousand Villages all include detailed narratives that allow consumers to align their identities with their purchases.[17]

Whereas handicraft sales provided an underpinning for the future success of fair trade, the market for mission-driven products was forever altered when "solidarity coffee" began to be imported to the United States. In a successful attempt to avoid a U.S.-imposed boycott of Nicaragua, the founders of Equal Exchange began shipping coffee to Holland and roasted it there. This "significantly altered" the product itself, and thus made it legal to import the beans to the United States. Or so the founders thought. The coffee was called "Café Nica, Nicaraguan Coffee, product of Holland." (Dutch trading laws required that "product of Holland" be included.) Alerted to the symbolic gesture of solidarity with Nicaraguan farmers, U.S. customs officials seized the first shipments of imported coffee. Equal Exchange's website recounts what happened: "During [the] first two years of business, the founders spent many days, with trade lawyers at their side, doing battle with customs officials. Each time the coffee cargo was released it was a small victory."[18] Although the initial growth of fair-trade coffee was slow, by the late 1990s, fair-trade sales had started to increase exponentially (see Table 1.1).

There are many reasons for this dramatic increase in sales. First, in 1989, the United States withdrew its support of the International Coffee Agreement (ICA). The ICA was ratified in 1963 and was supported by coffee growing and consuming countries around the world. The ICA was designed to raise and stabilize prices by establishing production quotas. Fearing the spread of communism and the instability of Central American countries during the Cold War, President John F. Kennedy viewed the ICA as playing an integral role in enhancing the economic development of Latin America.[19] By the late 1980s, however, the political and economic contexts of both the United States and Latin America had changed, and the United States withdrew from the ICA, citing uneven results of the agreement. The withdrawal of the United States led to the collapse of the ICA.

Table 1.1. Fair Trade Coffee Statistics 1998–2010

Year	Pounds Certified as Fair Trade
1998	76,059
1999	2,052,242
2000	4,249,534
2001	6,669,308
2002	9,747,571
2003	19,239,017
2004	32,974,400
2005	44,585,323
2006	64,774,431
2007	66,339,389
2008	87,772,966
2009	108,373,041
2010	108,928,751

Source: Fair Trade USA, "Fair Trade USA 2010 Almanac," 2011, electronic document, http://www.fairtradeusa.org/sites/default/files/Almanac% 202010_0.pdf, accessed October 31, 2011.

The ICA never tamed the fluctuation in coffee prices, but, after the agreement fell apart, price swings became much more dramatic.[20] After frost destroyed many of Brazil's coffee trees in the 1990s, the price of coffee reached a high of $3.05 a pound. This caught the attention of Vietnam, which was receiving significant redevelopment loans from the World Bank, and encouraged the country to significantly increase its coffee production. Between 1990 and 2000, Vietnam increased its coffee output by 1,400 percent, transitioning from a marginal coffee producer to the second leading exporter of coffee in the world.[21] As Vietnamese workers began to harvest the country's coffee crops, Brazil began to recover from its frost.[22] Around this same time, coffee production increased by more than 20 percent in India, Uganda, Guatemala, and Ethiopia.[23] The market became saturated, and, by 2001, the world market price of green coffee had fallen to just forty-one cents a pound.[24] The slew of bankrupt plantations led to widespread social problems throughout coffee-growing regions. The growing awareness of this coffee crisis lent credibility to fair-trade initiatives as a means to help impoverished farmers.[25]

Fair-trade coffee also grew because of the increase in the sale of specialty coffee. This "second wave" of coffee growth is characterized by the growth of the specialty coffee market, which is characterized by high-quality arabica beans. (The first wave was marked by the mainstreaming of cheap, robusta beans throughout the United States both before and after World War II.) The second wave began in the late 1960s with the founding of Peet's Coffee (1966) and, later, Starbucks (1971). Trish Skeie, a coffee consultant who popularized this "wave" idea, writes that the second wave continued through the mid-1990s.[26]

The mainstreaming of Starbucks helped to educate consumers about coffee quality and further expanded the market for independently owned coffee shops. By the early 1980s, writers were noting the parallels between the growth of specialty coffee and the growth of the wine industry.[27] In 1982, the Specialty Coffee Association of America (SCAA) was founded and began to actively grow the market for these higher-priced beans. Educated consumers, like wine connoisseurs before them, began to learn more and more about the factors that contribute to a good cup of coffee. With the focus shifting to the environments that produce higher-quality coffee, consumers also began to learn more about the farmers who grew their coffee. Just as it was becoming clear that consumers were more than willing to pay a price premium for specialty coffee, a collection of mission-driven entrepreneurs began promoting their socially conscious coffees.

Many observers are now claiming that the coffee market is in the midst of a third wave, where coffee is thought of as an artisanal good rather than as a commodity. The third wave began in the mid-1990s in response to the "McDonaldization" of the specialty coffee market.[28] Third-wavers rejected the search for the most rational and efficient means to produce high-quality coffee and rebelled against Starbucks' goal of purchasing the lowest quality of the high-end specialty coffee beans.[29] Instead, they traveled extensively to coffee-growing regions in search of the best beans available. They tried to outbid each other to purchase the beans of the winners of the coffee competitions such as the Cup of Excellence in Nicaragua. Representatives of prominent coffee companies like Counter Culture, Stumptown, La Colombe, and Intelligentsia take pride in their direct trading relationships with farmers and pay prices for beans that are much higher than fair-trade certification requires.[30] Many deploy the rhetoric associated with fair trade, even though their coffee is not necessarily certified as such.[31] I begin chapter 5 by showing how some coffee entrepreneurs compete for status with other importers who trade directly with the farmers who grow their beans.

During the last third of the twentieth century, more and more entrepreneurs entered fair-trade relationships. Both buyers and sellers sought a means to protect the integrity of this "socially conscious" form of trade. Independent labeling organizations were created to fulfill this need. Companies such as Max Havelar (1992) in the Netherlands and Fair Trade USA (1998, originally called TransFair USA) independently certify that organizations are trading according to fair-trade principles. They charge importers a small premium to attach a label certifying that their products are traded fairly and they charge farmers a fee to conduct the audit.[32] Fairtrade International (FLO) is an umbrella organization that coordinates fair-trade standards across countries, helps brand fair-trade products, and attempts to protect the purity of the movement. FLO also offers other, noneconomic benefits of fair-trade certification. It promotes environmentally friendly farming techniques and gender equity. Within the coffee market, it requires farmers to be members of democratically elected cooperatives where participation is open to all, regardless of political party, ethnic heritage, gender, or religion.

The goals of FLO are noble, but the organization itself has not avoided criticism. The rules used to enforce fair-trade standards have been criticized for being arbitrarily enforced and for lacking in transparency.[33] For instance, the anthropologist Sarah Lyon spent years interviewing and living alongside Maya coffee farmers in Guatemala. She found that FLO was unable to adequately audit whether or not fair trade was empowering women. Although auditors asked questions about gender issues in this community, they did not follow up to test the veracity of the claims made by the leaders of the cooperative, who were mostly men. Lyon argues that FLO should either stop claiming that fair trade is empowering women or come up with a more dynamic auditing process that can better assess fair trade's impact on women.[34]

A second criticism of FLO and fair-trade certification involves the reduction of the number of middlemen who skim profits along the coffee supply chain. Central American farmers, for instance, have long been at the whim of coffee "coyotes" who prey on some farmers' lack of knowledge about coffee quality and international prices. Coyotes, many

TransFair USA changed its name to Fair Trade USA despite widespread opposition. Cartoon by John Klossner, produced for Equal Exchange 2011.

fear, exploit farmers by setting artificially low coffee prices.[35] Although fair trade removes coyotes from the coffee supply chain, their place is taken by independent labeling organizations, which charge a fee to certify coffee as fair trade.[36] In essence, the exploitative middleman has been replaced by the do-gooder middleman.

Most recently, the bulk of consumer activists' ire has been directed at Fair Trade USA, which certifies that food entering the United States meets fair-trade standards. This conflict stems from Fair Trade USA's position in a marketplace that values both profits and social responsibility.[37] Although the roots of this conflict run much deeper, the mission-driven wing of the fair-trade movement really began to criticize TransFair USA when it changed its name to Fair Trade USA.

On September 16, 2010, TransFair USA announced the name change. Its press release stated, "The updated, simplified name and brand identity will support the organization's efforts to increase awareness of Fair Trade among a broader consumer audience, increase sales of Fair Trade Certified™ products, and generate more benefits for farmers and workers around the world."[38] The move came as a big surprise to many leading organizers in the fair-trade movement who had not been consulted about the change. As a result, the backlash was quick and fierce.

Equal Exchange, a seminal organization in the founding of the fair-trade movement, led a petition drive against the name change that gathered more than nine thousand signatures.[39] Phyllis Robinson, education and campaigns manager for Equal Exchange, conceded that the name change was a smart marketing strategy for Fair Trade USA but wrote:

> Fair Trade is a concept, a way of doing business, a value system, an entire movement built through the convictions and hard work of hundreds of thousands of individuals across the globe. Can one organization simply appropriate all that "Fair Trade" signifies, and claim it for itself?[40]

Similarly, Solidarity eXchange, an antisweatshop organization, extended this line of argument by distinguishing the goals of Fair Trade USA and other fair-trade organizations:

> They [Fair Trade USA] measure success by the number of producer lives that are improved even just a tiny bit, primarily monetarily. Many others in the fair trade movement value empowerment in a broader sense—not just through dollars and cents but through empowerment that looks like dignity through cooperative and union structures and living wages.[41]

The mission-driven wing of the fair-trade movement wanted to clarify the differences between Fair Trade USA, which it believes is too closely aligned with large profit-driven corporations such as Starbucks, and themselves. Its criticisms increased significantly in September 2011, when Fair Trade USA decided to end its relationship with FLO.

Paul Rice, CEO of Fair Trade USA, listed a number of reasons for dropping FLO certification and embarking on a new "vision" entitled "Fair Trade for All."[42] He first cited the inconsistencies in certification standards for different products and highlighted the differences for coffee, bananas, and tea. Whereas coffee must be grown on small, cooperatively run organizations, bananas and tea can be grown on "large farms." (Critics prefer the more provocative word "plantation.") He explained that removing these inconsistencies would allow more than four million farmers to gain access to the benefits associated with fair trade. Finally, the new Fair Trade for All aimed to greatly increase consumer awareness about fair trade initiatives. Paul wrote that more than 80 percent of consumers in Europe know what fair trade means, whereas only about 34 percent of Americans are familiar with the concept. Presumably, greater sales of fair-trade products would help educate consumers about the plight of farmers around the globe and thus better improve their living conditions.

This explanation, however, did not placate those who began to critique the decision immediately after it was announced in September 2011. Many lack trust in Fair Trade USA and fear that this powerful organization is again co-opting the meaning of fair trade. For instance, United Students for Fair Trade's press release formally withdrew the group's support for Fair Trade USA and explained that Fair Trade USA had recently lowered its standards for what constitutes fair trade. It cited the example of cocoa. Currently, a company can blend as little as 11 percent fair-trade cocoa with nonfair-trade cocoa and still receive certification. This, United Students for Fair Trade explained, is an "appallingly low" requirement.[43]

Other consumer activists fear that Fair Trade USA is working too closely with large corporations, which presumably care more about increasing profits and enhancing their brand image than improving the lives of farmers. Companies such as Walmart, Starbucks, and Nestlé have begun to sell fair-trade products, and Starbucks prominently displays the Fair Trade USA logo on advertisements even though less than 10 percent of its coffee is fair-trade certified.[44] Further, Starbucks' fair-trade beans are generally not brewed in most retail stores and are available only in whole-bean packages.[45] Nestlé also caught the ire of many fair-trade coffee-shop owners who sell 100 percent of their coffee according to fair-trade standards. In 2005, after ten years of arguing against all fair-trade initiatives, Nestlé introduced its Partner's Blend freeze-dried coffee into European markets. Advertised as the "coffee that helps farmers, their communities, and the environment," Partner's Blend is the only one out of more than 8,500 of Nestlé's products that is certified to carry a fair-trade logo.[46]

Another criticism of Fair Trade USA is that it does not include producers in its decision-making processes. Since at least 2005, when the first national fair-trade conference (called "Living a Fair Trade Life") was held in Chicago, major stakeholders in the movement have been asking that producers gain more representation on the board of Fair Trade USA. Many producers continue to claim that they are not being heard by this organization. The Alliance of Fair Trade Producer Networks (CAN), which represents more than eight hundred producer networks in sixty countries, publicly denounced Fair Trade USA's name-change decision.[47] Whereas CAN feels that it has a voice within FLO, it believes that it has little influence over Fair Trade USA's ability to decide what is right for CAN.

The most significant criticism of Fair Trade USA's decision to drop FLO certification was that it will hurt small-scale farmers. Rob Cameron, CEO of FLO, wrote that FLO "and the entire Fairtrade network sincerely regret Fair Trade USA's decision to pursue its own approach, rather than continue working within the global system." Because of the seasonal nature of coffee production, Cameron explained, Fair Trade USA will struggle to include transient workers into the democratically organized decision-making processes that are a requirement for FLO certification.[48] United Students for Fair Trade, a national network of student advocates, more directly confronted the problem:

> When 90% of cocoa producers and 70% of the world's coffee producers are small-scale farmers, many of whom would like to access Fair Trade markets, the argument that Fair Trade needs to source from plantations to expand is illogical.[49]

To compound this criticism, Ten Thousand Villages estimates that 80 percent of the coffee that could be certified as fair trade is sold through conventional markets.[50] In other words, the supply of fair-trade-certified coffee is currently outpacing demand, and many farmers are working under fair-trade standards but cannot find a buyer to purchase their coffee at fair-trade prices. Until worldwide demand for fair trade increases, there is no need to expand the certification criteria.

The tensions in the fair-trade marketplace are dynamic and will shape the future of this movement. Economic and cultural sociologists note the social factors that shape morality in these markets. As companies look to their peers' actions, they try to carve out a niche where their products can look distinct.[51] As I show throughout this book, consumers, activists, and entrepreneurs are also constantly competing for moral status within this marketplace. This competition for altruistic status has implications for brand reputation and profitability; most important, it will impact the well-being of farmers and artisans who directly benefit from fair-trade standards.

The Ethical Turn in Markets

The growth of the fair-trade movement is also the result of broader economic and sociocultural changes that have little to do with the movement itself. I refer to these changes, which have roughly occurred since the beginning of the twenty-first century, as an "ethical turn" in markets. This ethical turn is characterized by the mainstreaming of socially responsible products. This does not mean that these products are actually ethical but that they are advertised as being produced by ethical practices.[52] In fact, the debate over whether products are truly ethical is a central characteristic of the ethical turn. Thus, we begin to debate whether or not fair trade is more socially conscious than direct trade. To take an extreme example outside of fair trade, we begin to question whether products with known cancer-causing ingredients should be allowed to promote the Susan G. Komen's pink-ribbon campaign for cancer research.[53] In fact, a whole new vocabulary for criticizing corporate actions has developed as activists claim companies are "fairwashing," "sweatwashing," or "greenwashing" these movements, levying these charges against corporations that do not appear to be following through with their sustainable claims or that are making only superficial changes to their ethical practices.[54]

As part of this ethical turn, consumers are increasingly concerned with who made the products they bought, how the producer benefits from the sale of the object, and how the environment is impacted throughout the life course of the object.[55] Retail sales of a wide range of so-called ethical products are increasing; examples include fair-trade products, pink-ribbon-endorsed products, Newman's Own line of food, hybrid cars, energy-efficient light bulbs, Product(RED)[56] and other "green" products. Consumers seem to be increasingly motivated to seek out products where the proceeds go to charitable and altruistic causes. The ethical turn means that even mainstream consumers and mainstream corporations are starting to consider social responsibility as a criterion when they make market decisions.

The origins of the ethical turn stem from a long history of civic responsibility within markets. Lizabeth Cohen, author of *A Consumers' Republic*, explains that Americans have long sought social change through shopping.[57] The boycott of British tea and fabrics prior to the American Revolution is an often-cited instance of consumer activism. The Montgomery bus boycotts during the Civil Rights Movement is another. During the 1930s, Americans started to become "more self-conscious about their identities and interests as consumers."[58] At this time, a tension between people's roles as citizens and as consumers began to arise. The citizen consumer was responsible for "safeguarding the general good of the nation, in particular for prodding government to protect the rights, safety, and fair treatment of individual consumers in the private marketplace," whereas the purchasing consumer contributed to society "more by exercising purchasing power than through asserting themselves politically."[59] The tension between those who believe that all shopping serves as a means of economic development (consumer as purchaser) and those who believe that there is a morally correct way to shop (consumer as citizen) are evident in the framing of free-trade versus fair-trade initiatives. In many ways, contemporary consumer-dependent social movements (e.g., fair trade, organic, pink ribbon) are a rejuvenated version of the citizen consumer movement.[60] There are many reasons for this "ethical turn" in markets.

Increasing awareness about the sustainability of our consumption patterns is the simplest explanation for the ethical turn. We can learn about global warming from Al Gore's Oscar-winning documentary *An Inconvenient Truth* (2006), calculate our carbon footprint on a number of different websites, or find out about the ill effects of our consumption patterns by reading Annie Leonard's book *The Story of Stuff* (2010).[61] (Her film with the same title has been viewed more than twelve million times online.) Even popular films for children such as Pixar's *WALL-E* and Dreamworks' *Over the Hedge* have framed overconsumption as a social problem that needs a solution.

Juliet Schor's book *True Wealth* provides the scientific evidence to back up claims about the dangers of shopping made by many within the mainstream media.[62] Schor, taking a creative approach to the issue, examines the percentage increase in the weight of imports of a wide range of products from 1998 to 2007. During the nine-year period leading up to the Great Recession of 2008, the weight of many imports increased by some staggering rates: 155 percent for furniture; 75 percent for electronics such as computers, MP3 players, cell phones, and televisions; 83 percent for ceramics; 59 percent for toys and games; and 70 percent for textiles. The numbers become a bit more frightening when you factor in the environmental impacts of producing, shipping, and ultimately disposing of these products. Schor shows that many products are moving in and out of style faster than ever before. As a result, individuals who want to stay in style must buy the latest clothing, electronics, and even furniture. Cheap, stylish furniture from stores like IKEA spurs consumers to buy more fashionable sofas, and rapid technological advances encourage desires for the newest electronic devices. Schor convincingly argues that this path leads in only one direction: planetary ecocide.

Many consumers, perhaps prodded by those working in the so-called culture industries, are seeking to remedy these environmental problems through shopping. Sales of hybrid cars, halogen and LED lights, rain barrels, and eco-friendly water bottles are all booming.[63] Shoppers can now find eco-friendly alternatives to conventional automobile oil, home cleaning products, beauty products, lawn-care products, and even toothbrushes. Many companies are jumping on the green bandwagon by rebranding their conventional products as eco-friendly. A few have even created their own green standards and certified their own line of products to meet these standards.[64] This growing concern for the environment, whether sincere or simply profit driven, has led to a somewhat unexpected phenomenon: going green has become trendy.

Of course, buying products to obtain social status is not a new phenomenon. Thorstein Veblen, author of *The Theory of the Leisure Class*, famously described the upper-class's ability to demonstrate its social position through conspicuous consumption, conspicuous waste, and conspicuous leisure.[65] But, of course, times have changed. In this more global era, products do not convey similar meanings across large populations. So, whereas buying a Hummer may be a sign of high social status in some networks, it is looked upon with disfavor in others. For a long time, this is what happened in markets that promoted social responsibility. Many consumers took pride in attempting to change the world by subscribing to the countercultural magazine *Whole Earth Catalogue* or by shopping at Whole Foods.[66] But outsiders viewed this type of consumption as economically irrational or even pretentious. Ethical consumption acted as a form of "symbolic violence," a means for one group to convey to another that there is a correct way to shop.[67]

The rules for gaining status among ethical shopping are changing as ethical products reach a broader audience. Malcolm Gladwell, in his best-selling book *The Tipping Point*, describes one of the ways trends go viral even without the backing of large advertising campaigns. Some fads spread because "cool" people endorse products in the right space at the right time.[68] Within the ethical-consumption marketplace, Lance Armstrong's yellow Livestrong bracelets are the quintessential example of a product that went viral.

In 1997, after being diagnosed with testicular cancer, Armstrong founded the Lance Armstrong Foundation with the goal of helping to improve the lives of individuals who are affected by cancer. In 2004, the foundation began selling plastic yellow wristbands at Niketown Outlets, Footlocker stores, and other retailers to support cancer research. Seventy cents from each one-dollar band was donated to cancer research. John Kerry, Katie Couric, Matt Damon, and, of course, Armstrong were all photographed wearing the bracelets throughout the year. By 2005, more than fifty-five million people had bought the bracelets. They became so popular that other causes created colorful wristbands of their own; eBay began trading the bracelets for up to $10 (even though these profits did not go to charity), and knock-off yellow bands even popped up at flea-markets and underground markets throughout the United States.[69] Some people took pride in supporting cancer research, others sought a marker of social status, and still others wanted to feel a part of something bigger than themselves.[70]

Around this same time, in 2004, the Toyota Prius began to hit a tipping point of its own. The Prius first appeared in the United States in the summer of 2000, but dealers were initially very skeptical about the car's potential for success. They were fearful that environmentalists would be reluctant to purchase the car and were leery of the car's design. (Although the design of the Prius changed dramatically in 2003, the car remained visibly distinct from other vehicles). Larry Miller, who owned nine Toyota and Lexus dealerships around Salt Lake City, Utah, told CNN in 2006 that he thought that the car's design was simply "passable" and acknowledged that he hoped "it wouldn't embarrass us."[71] The design became a marker of identity for the conscientious consumers, and is now viewed as a primary reason why the Toyota Prius has outsold the more conventionally designed hybrid Honda Civic.[72] Whereas sales of the Civic stagnated, dealers had six-month waitlists for the comparable Toyota Prius. In focus groups, customers said they wanted an eco-friendly hybrid car, but they also wanted others to know they were driving a hybrid car. Going green was becoming a trendy marker of social status.[73]

As more consumers began purchasing socially responsible products, the cost of producing many of these products began to decrease. As any student in an introductory economics course can explain, this decrease is due to economies of scale. Producing one vehicle is incredibly expensive, but, because of the greater efficiencies involved in the production process when many cars are being produced, the cost of manufacturing each subsequent vehicle is reduced. As a result, producing large numbers of goods tends to drive down prices. Today, many consumers are buying energy-efficient light bulbs and solar panels for their homes, not because they care about going green but because they care about saving money. Thus, even consumers who couldn't care less about buying green are becoming attracted to the idea of saving money.[74]

Another stimulus for the ethical turn involves the price of oil. Environmentalists have long cited dependence on oil as a social problem associated with high carbon emissions and the potential for catastrophic oil spills. The 2010 BP oil spill in the Gulf of Mexico reignited the fears of environmentalists. But the spikes in oil prices over the past ten years, largely due to instability in the Middle East, have increased the number of individuals advocating for cleaner energy. Oil dependency is now viewed as a social problem by a wider swath of Americans than in the past; those concerned about rising shipping costs or national security issues are aligning themselves with the concerns of environmentalists. As gas prices surpassed the $4.00-a-gallon mark in the spring of 2008 and the cost of home heating oil surged, the mass media focused increased attention on alternatives: electric cars, hybrid engines, solar panels, and geothermal energy. For a brief period, pressure in Congress for alternative energy sources began to mount. And at least some consumers, seeing the spectacle of oil-covered birds in the Gulf of Mexico, started to rethink their own spending habits.[75]

A final but extremely important reason for the growth of ethical consumption stems from Americans' loss of faith in the federal government. In the months following the attacks of September 11, 2001, more than 60 percent of Americans said they "just about always" or "most of the time" had trust in the "government in Washington." But as the United States entered wars in Afghanistan and Iraq, trust in government began to plunge. By March 2010, following the Great Recession and the bank bailouts and in the midst of high unemployment, only 22 percent of Americans said they always or mostly trusted the government in Washington, D.C.[76]

As Americans became increasingly frustrated with their government, whether because of the wars in Iraq or Afghanistan, the U.S. Supreme Court decision that ended the 2000 election recounts, or the constant attacks about governmental corruption from members of the Tea Party, they turned to create change through markets. Their lack of faith in government policies and leadership (both at home and abroad) does not mean that Americans have given up, as some have suggested.[77] Instead, they have sought to express their ideals at the point of purchase.[78] Frustrated by the lack of funding for cancer research, they buy a cup of Alex's lemonade; concerned with the deleterious effects of AIDS in Africa, they purchase a RED-certified T-shirt; tired of seeing impoverished coffee farmers struggling with the aftereffects of the coffee crisis, they organize their morning ritual around a cup of Equal Exchange coffee. They might not be able to elect a politician who shares their same values, but they can feel that they are creating a more socially just world through shopping.

Whereas all these factors clearly led to the ethical turn in American markets, it is fair to question how these factors influenced the fair-trade market. For instance, fair-trade farmers and artisans do not benefit from the economies of scale present in the automobile industry. Nevertheless, I believe that the fair-trade market benefits greatly from the momentum of these other markets and movements. The faddish success of the Livestrong bracelets and the cult-like devotion of Prius owners are infectious. There seems to be a spillover effect from one movement (or market) to another. Seeing that others are shopping responsibly and learning about the funds being raised to support cancer research, AIDS treatments, and fair-trade farmers, consumers come to believe that shopping can make a difference in the world.[79]

It is within this context (growing awareness of consumption as a social problem, declining trust in government, record high oil prices, trendiness and enhanced status associated with purchasing ethical products, and lower prices due to economies of scale) that I describe the culture of ethical consumption in Philadelphia. Before outlining the chapters that follow, I will describe my research methods.

An Ethnography of Shopping

In order to gain a greater comprehension of how consumers understand the meaning of fair trade and ethical consumption, I started spending time in fair-trade retail stores throughout Philadelphia. Most of these shops are located in college towns or urban areas, so Philadelphia provided a convenient space to conduct much of my research. I collected both interview and ethnographic data from a Ten Thousand Villages store and from a cooperative of fair-trade coffee shops called Independents. There are more than 160 Ten Thousand Villages retail stores in the United States and Canada, making the organization the largest retailer of fair-trade handicrafts in the world.[80] Independents, by contrast, was a small for-profit cooperative formed in order to better advertise member coffee shops and to buy coffee and other items in bulk at lower prices. Members of this fair-trade coffee cooperative chose the name "Independents" to stress that their stores were all independently owned. The name also plays off Philadelphia's historical connections with the Declaration of Independence. Although most of the founders of Independents continue to work in the coffee market, the cooperative formally disbanded in November 2010. I provide more detailed information about each of the four original Independents' coffeehouses in the Appendix: the Greenline Café (West Philadelphia), Infusion Coffee and Tea (Mount Airy), Joe Coffee Bar (Center City), and Mugshots Coffeehouse and Café (Art Museum).

For almost two years, I visited fair-trade handicraft and coffee shops throughout Philadelphia. I volunteered at a Ten Thousand Villages store

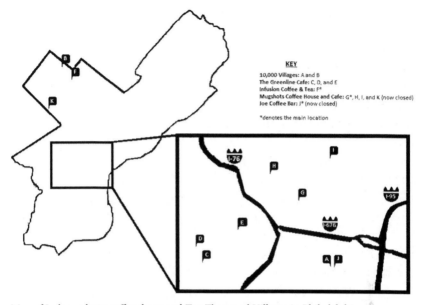

KEY

10,000 Villages: A and B
The Greenline Cafe: C, D, and E
Infusion Coffee & Tea: F*
Mugshots Coffee House and Cafe: G*, H, I, and K (now closed)
Joe Coffee Bar: J* (now closed)

*denotes the main location

Map of Independents coffee shops and Ten Thousand Villages in Philadelphia.

and gathered ethnographic data at the four original Independents coffee shops. Each week I worked as a retail clerk at Ten Thousand Villages in order to see what the best-selling products are, how fair-trade products are framed to attract consumers, and how consumers construct the meanings of fair trade during face-to-face interactions with retail staff. At coffee shops, I took note of how retailers discussed fair trade with consumers. I also attended the Independents cooperative meetings during which members chose the cooperative's logo, discussed how to advertise the organization, and planned how to minimize costs by buying in bulk. These meetings provided insight into the framing strategies used to advertise and promote a socially responsible organization. They also helped me understand how coffee-shop owners make financial decisions that are related to social responsibility.

In sum, I conducted 103 interviews with local and national leaders of the fair-trade movement, consumers, store owners, and store managers. Most of these interviews lasted between one and two hours. In order to protect the privacy of these respondents and to encourage them to speak candidly with me, the names of people I interviewed for this project have been changed. (Joe Cesa, whom I introduce later, is the lone exception. He wanted to be publicly identified in this book.) Twenty seven of the interviews were conducted with a research team trying to assess the current state and future direction of the fair-trade movement. For these interviews, I was hired by the Fair Trade Research Network to conduct and analyze interviews over the phone with nationally recognized leaders of fair trade. I sat in on a conference in Baltimore, Maryland, with these interviewees as they discussed the future of the movement. I was therefore privy to some provocative debates about the limits and possibilities of fair trade.

In addition, I attended the Living a Fair Trade Life conference in Chicago, Illinois; Ten Thousand Villages' employee workshop in Ephrata, Pennsylvania; and the reality tour to Nicaragua with which I opened this chapter. In each instance, I sought to understand the social forces that lead individuals to identify as ethical consumers. (In the Appendix, I describe my research methods in more detail.)

Becoming an Ethical Consumer

I begin chapter 2 by introducing Joe Cesa, the owner of Philadelphia's first fair-trade coffee shop. He is a staple of Philadelphia's movement for socially responsible shopping. He may not be the most high-profile member (that honor likely goes to Judy Wicks, the founder of the Sustainable Business Network and the White Dog Café), but he played a pivotal role in expanding awareness about fair trade. I describe the factors that led Joe to vigorously support fair trade and describe the obstacles he faced in trying to run a profitable, socially responsible business. As his business began to falter, Joe cultivated his reputation as a moral entrepreneur through his unwavering support of local, organic, and fair-trade initiatives. Joe's experiences in fair trade will likely resonate with those who are interested in understanding how financial decisions are made in a context where social responsibility is highly valued. After concentrating on Joe's experiences in chapter 2, I take a broader look at the different types of fair-trade consumers and the pathways that led them to support these initiatives.

When I began to interview people who shop at fair-trade stores, I learned that consumers adopt one of three types of roles while searching for ethical products. These roles reflect different types of shopping patterns: (1) *promoters*, a small but very active group of store owners, managers, fair-trade NGO employees, and consumer activists who organize all their purchases around "social responsibility," (2) *conscientious consumers*, who like to buy fair-trade and other socially responsible products but are not committed to organizing all of their purchasing decisions around this belief system, and (3) *purchasers*, a group of consumers who know little about fair trade but buy the products because of aesthetics, price, taste, or utility.

The promoters are at the center of the fair-trade movement, influencing its direction at local and national levels, encouraging stores to carry fair-trade commodities, and recommending fair-trade products to other consumers. Many are vegetarians, most try to buy local and organic food, and all say they avoid big-chain stores like Walmart and Starbucks. They view themselves as part of a movement and see all forms of consumption as having political and ethical implications. Promoters are members of a wide range of organizations that advocate socially responsible consumption. Most began supporting the fair-trade movement after being greatly impacted by a travel experience to a developing country. Promoters are largely from the upper-middle class and strongly believe that their decisions in the marketplace help to alleviate global inequalities.

Ashley, for example, is a passionate fair-trade promoter who shares many of the core beliefs of this group. She is a thirty-two-year-old social activist and a member of a large nonprofit organization that promotes fair trade. She has traveled to Mexico, India, Venezuela, Kenya, Brazil, Cuba, Iraq, Japan, and most countries in Central America and Western Europe. Ashley grew up in an upper-middle-class suburb of New York City and realized all the privileges she had only after traveling to Mexico on a high-school exchange program. After that trip, she explained, "a light bulb just went on that it wasn't fair. . . . It wasn't fair that me and my brother had all of these opportunities and that other people didn't." Around this time, Ashley realized she wanted to support workers in developing countries, and, a few years later, she joined a large nonprofit working to educate consumers about fair trade. She spent her vacation in 2006 living on a fair-trade farm in northern Nicaragua. In chapter 3, I describe more of the processes and extraordinary experiences that led Ashley and her fellow promoters to begin supporting fair trade.

Conscientious consumers constitute the bulk of the fair-trade consumers that I met. These consumers buy fair-trade products when they are readily available and will occasionally go a little out of their way to shop responsibly. Like promoters, they tend to be highly educated, upper-middle-class consumers. Many said they would pay a bit more for fair-trade, organic, or locally produced products. They differ from the promoters in that they do not see themselves as part of a larger movement and do not partake in the rituals or consciousness-building activities that serve to foster a fair-trade identity. Nonetheless, these are critical consumers who routinely think about the origin of the products they buy and who made them. These consumers are more prone to "impulse shopping" than promoters and admit to contradictory shopping patterns, often buying products that do not align with their own ideals. Many conscientious consumers began buying fair-trade products after receiving a fair-trade gift or learning about the movement while frequenting a fair-trade coffee shop or a Ten Thousand Villages retail store.

Other than her class background, Melissa shares many of the characteristics of conscientious consumers. She grew up in a working-class neighborhood in western Maryland but now lives in Mount Airy, a Philadelphia neighborhood that is one of the most racially diverse neighborhoods in the United States. The *New York Times* columnist David Brooks would likely refer to Mount Airy as a home of the so-called Bobos, bourgeois bohemian individuals of the new upper class who embody both the radical values of the 1960s and the enterprising, "yuppie" (young, urban, professional) values of the 1980s.[81] Melissa and her immediate family shop at Walmart, but she says that her friends "harass me mercilessly about shopping at Walmart, all of them. They're horrible." Melissa likes the positive feelings she gets from patronizing the local fair-trade coffee shop and from buying gifts at Ten Thousand Villages, but she is very price conscious and shops at Walmart so that she can afford to buy other socially responsible products:

> I know it's crazy. It's crazy. Going to Walmart allows me to have the money to then spend at Whole Foods. And Whole Foods has really strict policies about the kind of food that they'll sell. . . . Then when my husband says, "Oh my God! You spent a dollar for an orange?" I'm like,

"Well, I only spent $5 on a shirt at Walmart." It's a lot easier to justify why I'm spending money.

Melissa is acutely aware of the contradictions in her purchasing patterns. She earmarks her money and views socially responsible food as a more important purchase than antisweatshop clothing. Many of the conscientious consumers claimed a strong dislike for chain stores or fast-food restaurants but then confided that they still occasionally frequent these types of stores. In chapter 4, I describe the moral contradictions that conscientious consumers face when trying to align their values with their everyday purchases. I show how they manage to maintain their identities as conscientious consumers, even when so many of their everyday purchases seem to contradict this sense of self.

Most of the purchasers know little to nothing about fair trade. These consumers enter an Independents coffee shop looking for a good cup of coffee or walk into a Ten Thousand Villages looking for a unique gift. Many identify as big shoppers and consider taste, aesthetics, price, and utility as the primary criteria guiding their consumption patterns. The majority of these consumers could not explain what fair trade means and were hesitant to speak with me about the issue. This is a diverse group of consumers who are not as easily classifiable as the first two groups. Because their lives are not organized around socially responsible consumption, it is more difficult to ascertain their motivations for shopping at fair-trade retail stores. Some are looking for handicrafts representing their ethnic heritage, others desire a unique gift, a few want to patronize an independently owned coffee shop, and a small percentage are simply looking for a last-minute gift idea.

Terry is a fifty-two-year-old purchaser who works for a nonprofit organization. She began buying handicrafts from Ten Thousand Villages after window-shopping in Chestnut Hill. She lives with her boyfriend in an apartment in a racially diverse working-class neighborhood in Philadelphia and does not think of herself as an ethical consumer. She has a hard time grasping what fair trade means but acknowledges that she knows the money she spends at Ten Thousand Villages supports producers in developing countries. Terry's primary motivation for shopping at Ten Thousand Villages is that she can find products that are "unique" and "can't be found anywhere else." She proudly displays a "tree of life" wall hanging in her apartment but does not mention to her friends where the product came from or who made it. I discuss purchasers in this book, but the bulk of *Buying into Fair Trade* focuses on the experiences of promoters and conscientious consumers in the fair-trade movement.

Altruistic Shoppers? Well, Sometimes

Once I began to understand more about the different roles that fair-trade consumers play in the marketplace, I sought to answer a question that kept confounding me: why are individuals so reluctant to talk about the ethical implications of shopping? After all, fair-trade retail stores are filled with advertisements explaining how fair trade helps farmers and artisans. All of the stores have pictures of smiling farmers and artisans who are "empowered" by making fair-trade products. Ten Thousand Villages even displays a sign with a quotation from two artisans from El Salvador: "With each product you buy, there is one more tortilla for our families." But consumers often avoided talking about ethics, morality, and fair trade. Instead, they often reframed conversations around a product's price, utility, quality, or aesthetics. Even the most steadfast fair-trade promoters often steered conversations away from ethical issues.

In chapter 5, I take a deeper look at the strategies that shoppers deploy to position themselves as altruistic. Writing in the vein of a "how to" book, I describe the rules that conscientious consumers must follow in order to appear altruistic. Consumers must talk self-righteously about the merits of boycotting market leaders like Walmart, Nike, and the Gap. But they must not go overboard in critiquing "fairwashing" companies like Starbucks, a place that they occasionally like to frequent. The goal is to talk skeptically about the veracity of Starbucks' claims to be a socially responsible and environmentally friendly coffee shop. Those consumers who really want to appear altruistic need to tell exotic stories about far-off coffee farmers. As conscientious consumers tell these stories, they must avoid coming off as "too preachy." They need to avoid conflict with the people with whom they are interacting and seek ways to converse that won't alienate their peers.

This "How to" chapter takes a somewhat polemical position on socially responsible consumption. I do this intentionally, as I seek to redirect our attention away from the status-seeking dimension of ethical consumption and toward the real, material implications of our everyday purchases. If consumers want to get serious about enacting social change through the marketplace, I argue, they need to adopt a much more radical approach to shopping.

The Social Significance of Shopping

Lately, many journalists and fair-trade supporters have begun to cite survey research showing that a majority of consumers say they will pay a premium for goods that are produced "ethically." These surveys are cited as a reason to become optimistic about changes in the ways Americans are consuming.[82] But, as I show throughout this book, these survey responses do not tell the whole story. While many enjoy the status associated with looking like a "socially responsible" consumer, these same individuals are still greatly concerned with issues such as price, convenience, aesthetics, and product quality. This more "instrumentalist" orientation toward markets strongly governs the ways individuals understand, talk about, and shop for fair-trade products. And even the most steadfast fair-trade supporters manage a tension between their ethical and their instrumentalist orientations toward markets. By earmarking some purchases as ethical and others as instrumental, consumers are able to maintain their ethical image of themselves while ignoring moral standards when shopping for other products.[83]

In my concluding chapter, "The Great Recession and the Social Significance of Buying into Fair Trade," I examine the limits and possibilities of ethical consumption. I begin by discussing how Philadelphia's fair-trade handicraft and coffee shops are coping with the dramatic changes in the American economy. For example, whereas a few coffee shops permanently closed their doors, in part because of the economy, others are opening new cafés in Philadelphia. I then discuss the pros and cons of ethical consumption. A growing number of scholars are beginning to ask whether shopping ethically encourages consumers to think differently about their everyday purchases: does it motivate them to seek out other socially responsible goods? Does it act as a gateway to social activism? Does it discourage other forms of charitable giving? Or does it simply relieve the guilt consumers feel from their other, more exploitative purchases? I weigh in on these debates and write about the cultural stigmas attached to the fair-trade movement. I also discuss the tenuous nature of ethical consumption, pointing to the wide range of consumers who justify their support of and movement away from socially responsible products in terms of the amount of money they can save.

I was often greatly inspired by the optimism displayed by the people I spoke with in the fair-trade movement. I couldn't keep myself from nodding in agreement when interviewees spoke about the potential to change the world through shopping. I found myself swayed by what I call the "fantasy of choice" argument deployed by many: if given the choice of two equal products, I will always choose the socially responsible option. Unfortunately, this optimism was countered by the harsher reality that consumer practices often do not align with consumer ideals. Yes, most people want to feel good about buying ethically, but these same individuals admit to countless contradictions in which their ideals do not match their everyday purchases. These contradictions abound within the marketplace for socially responsible products and are discussed in great depth in the chapters that follow. Consumers' ability to reconcile these contradictions will impact the future direction of markets for ethical products. While their words often inspire, consumers make everyday purchases that raise the question of whether our current capitalist markets will ever become more altruistic.

2

"Just One Normal Coffee"

Crafting Joe's Moral Reputation

"Can I just get a regular cup of coffee?" the frustrated and caffeine-deprived woman asked upon entering Joe's café for the first (and probably last) time. "I've had the organic-type coffee before, and I don't want anything like that." Joe, who was working the counter, blushed. He assured the woman that he sold only the "highest quality" coffee beans picked by workers who "are paid fairly." He even added one of his oft-repeated but not entirely true refrains: "No children picked the beans in this coffee."[1] But the customer did not look convinced, so Joe exclaimed, "Ma'am, just have a cup of coffee. If you don't like it, I'll buy it back from you." The customer relented. "Okay, just one *normal* coffee."

In the spring of 2006, Joe told me that his customers are slowly becoming aware of what fair-trade and organic certifications mean. "I believe I'm doing the right thing [selling fair trade and organic], but I must be out of my mind. I'm too far ahead of the curve. I'm trying to move the planet and get the country to recognize fair trade, and people don't know what the fuck I'm talking about." Joe's frustration is shared by many mission-driven fair-trade entrepreneurs. At Ten Thousand Villages, for instance, volunteers and managers take great pride in their ability to sell handicrafts and coffee that support some of the most impoverished people in the world. They justify their volunteer status and low pay by feeling that they are making a difference in the world. But this pride is challenged when customers complain about prices, aesthetics, or small defects in the quality of a handicraft.

This chapter examines how Joe, the owner of Philadelphia's first fair-trade coffee shop, tries to manage the tensions between running a profitable business and advocating for fair-trade and other social-justice initiatives. It focuses on Joe, not because he is representative of other fair-trade entrepreneurs but because he played a seminal role in the growth of Philadelphia's emphasis on socially responsible consumption. Joe helped found a cooperative of fair-trade café owners, hosted farmers from Latin America in his shop, traveled to meet and live alongside farmers in Puerto Rico and Nicaragua, and funded developmental initiatives for farmers in Peru. He gained national attention for his support of health-care initiatives in the United States, meeting with U.S. senators, speaking in front of city hall, and being mentioned in a front-page article in USA Today.[2] He was even given a national "local leadership" award by Green America for his role in promoting fair trade. In essence, he has established a well-regarded reputation as a socially responsible entrepreneur within Philadelphia.

All this success in supporting social-justice initiatives, however, did not lead to a more profitable business. And, after more than seven years in business, Joe closed the doors to his café in May 2009. This chapter explains how Joe justified working so hard on fair-trade and other progressive initiatives while his own store was failing to become economically viable. Many economists and, as I explain, even auditors from the Internal Revenue Service would struggle to explain why Joe kept his store open for so long. But social-movement theorists provide great insight here. Joe was motivated by what they call an "alternative reward system."[3] Rather than seeking financial gains, he kept working hard because of the positive recognition he received during everyday interactions, from the attention his shop received in the media, and from the strong social networks of like-minded entrepreneurs. His motivation to

Joe Cesa speaking in front of city hall at "Uninsured Americans Week" in May 2005. His advocacy paid off; he eventually received some health insurance benefits in 2012 due to President Obama's health care changes.

keep his café open, or what a few sympathetic small-business owners called his "foolishness," was rooted in his belief that his coffee shop was helping to change the world.

Born into Coffee

Joe Cesa was born into a first-generation Italian family in a small Italian neighborhood in Northeast Philadelphia. "Everyone spoke Italian around me. That's the basic language, and coffee was always a part of [that]." One of Joe's earliest memories is of sitting with his mother at a neighbor's house. He was only three years old at the time, but he recalls his mother setting out a tiny cup for him to sip from. "It was . . . mostly warm milk," but it had a "little coffee."

In 1978, Joe finally got a chance to visit Italy. He was in his late twenties and wanted to learn more about his family history and Italian culture. One thing that stuck out in his mind from that trip was the coffee culture in Italy. "I knew this before I went over; coffee's a really big part of their life. They have these little bars, and you get breakfast in Italy at a bar. A bar is completely different than what you see here." Joe quickly realized that this was the type of shop he wanted to open.[4] But he was not yet prepared to start his own business.

In 1989, Joe opened a small catering business in West Philadelphia. It took off, and he soon wanted to expand to also serve customers in a café. "So I saw this little tiny restaurant tucked away, and I was going to turn it into a coffeehouse. And I thought if it doesn't make a lot of money, it doesn't matter, because all of this stuff I'm using for the catering business. What does it cost to make a little carrot cake after I've made a big carrot cake?" Whereas Joe's catering business continued to expand, the small café was not as fortunate.

"Nobody had any idea what the hell I was doing," Joe explained to me during our first formal interview. He intended to sell only coffee and pastries, but, as he explains in his reenactment of countless conversations, customers did not understand the Italian-inspired philosophy of the café:

> "That's it? But why?"
>> "Well, it's like a European bar," Joe would respond.
> "Are you going to have liquor?"
> "No, it's going to be a bar but without liquor."
> "Well, what do you do?"
> "You drink coffee . . . and you talk with your friends."
> "I can do that at home."
> "Yeah, but you don't have to do it at home. Don't you get tired of just sitting in the house? So come out. You don't have to wash the dishes when you're done. You drink better coffee than you drink at home."

The café and catering business closed after five years. Joe told me his customers "just didn't get it." But there was another reason this business did not succeed. Joe's best friend had a terminal illness, and he spent countless hours cleaning his friend's home, caring for him, and driving him to his doctors' appointments. "And by the end, I was burned out. The restaurant was a shadow of what it was. And I was barely functional. . . . I'd be forgetting things. And then one night I went in . . .

and I went to grab a [hot] pan with my bare hand. It's like you just can't function." Between caring for his friend and running his catering business, Joe was working sixteen- or seventeen-hour days, six days a week. Every seventh day, he slept. As his business suffered and his friend passed away, Joe decided to close his shop. In the years following, he worked as a specialty-foods buyer in the Italian market and as a food-services director at a health-care facility. But his desire to reopen a coffee shop never faded.

In the late 1990s, Joe felt the time was right to try again. Starbucks was becoming incredibly successful, and Americans had proved they were willing to pay a premium price for specialty coffee. Coffee shops were filling a much-needed function in that they acted as a community meeting place at a time when Americans' civic participation was decreasing.[5] Joe began learning more about coffee by talking with local café owners and attending trade shows. It was through these experiences that he first heard about fair trade.

About three years prior to opening this second shop, Joe attended a coffee trade show in Seattle, Washington. He kept hearing members of Fair Trade USA (at the time it was called TransFair USA) and the Specialty Coffee Association of America complaining about Starbucks. Although most of the conference focused on coffee quality (production, harvesting, the five grades of coffee beans), much attention kept coming back to Starbucks. Many were asking why Starbucks refused to sell fair-trade-certified coffee. The debate was turning nasty as representatives from Starbucks replied that fair trade was not their problem. Activists were talking about the "coffee crisis" in Central America and the fact that the price of coffee beans was plummeting to less than a dollar a pound for green beans. (Green beans have not been roasted). Stories of malnutrition, unemployment, and mass migrations in Central America were beginning to permeate the conference. But Joe felt he still didn't have enough information about fair trade to make an informed decision.

Nevertheless, he kept educating himself about the plight of coffee farmers. He began to feel that the coffee crisis was getting worse. And, around this same time, fourteen immigrants from Veracruz, a coffee-growing state within Mexico, died from heat exposure while trying to cross the border into Arizona. This story had a profound impact on Joe.

"They were all coffee farmers. And they were smuggling themselves into the country because they [couldn't] make [a] living on their coffee farm, and they just gave up."[6] Joe said he kept hearing about these earth-friendly coffees, and he kept "seeing this movement" for fair trade. He believed it could make a difference in the lives of farmers like the ones who had died while crossing the border into Arizona. He eventually decided to use Equal Exchange for 70 to 80 percent of his coffee and Torreo, a family-owned coffee company that he trusted, for the remainder.

Once he committed to Equal Exchange and fair trade, Joe remained a bit uneasy about his decision, telling me, "I wasn't really certain this is where I wanted to go." He talked with friends about his decision to sell fair-trade and organic coffee in 2001, and none of them truly supported his decision. They said, "Don't put a sign up [promoting fair trade and organic]" (which he did) and "Don't go telling people" about these issues (which he also did). During the first year he was open, Joe remembers working "like a dog" and then taking a Sunday afternoon off, when he bumped into an old acquaintance:

> And we're both running into the movie at the last minute. And [he asks], "What are you doing?"
> And I told him [about my café].
> "Oh, and you're doing food. What's different about your coffee?"
> And I told him about the fair-trade coffee. And he made some remark about lesbians.
> And I just thought—fair trade. Organic. Lesbians. Birkenstocks. It's just like the stereotype. You must have big bowls of granola, complimentary granola on the counter. And it's just like, Fuck, this is stupid. It just annoys me.

Joe's fears about the stereotypes surrounding fair trade were a bit exaggerated but definitely legitimate. While a growing number of entrepreneurs were opening small stores selling ethically sourced handicrafts, clothing, and food, mainstream consumers were lagging behind. Years later, when I interviewed fair-trade consumers between 2004 and 2007, most still had a very loose understanding of what fair trade meant. They would tell me things like, "The farmers make more

Few café owners in Philadelphia included signs promoting their "fair-trade" and "organic" coffees. Joe initially struggled to get some of his customers to understand what fair trade and organic mean. Photo by Pamela Lowe.

money." They trusted store owners like Joe, but they did not understand what the logos for Fair Trade USA or the World Fair Trade Organization (WFTO) meant (Fair Trade USA certifies products as fair trade, whereas WFTO certifies organizations as fair trade). In 2012, Fair Trade USA's latest surveys estimate that only 34 percent of Americans were familiar with the term "fair trade."[7] When Joe became frustrated with customers who did not know what fair trade meant, he could talk about fair-trade, environmental, and labor initiatives with a growing group of like-minded entrepreneurs—the Sustainable Business Network (SBN).

Right around the time Joe opened the doors of his café, Judy Wicks was founding the SBN in Philadelphia. The SBN is composed of business owners who support a triple bottom line of people, planet, and profit. Wicks became a nationally recognized leader in the sustainable and locally sourced food communities. She opened her pioneering restaurant, the White Dog Café, in 1983. At the time, her goal was simply to create a successful business. She believed she could then use her profits to support social causes that she cared about. In her own words, she felt that she needed to "do well before" she could "do good." But she soon realized that her life was her business. She didn't have time to do much of anything but run her restaurant. She realized it was time to incorporate her own values into her own business.

"Business is about relationships," Wicks proudly proclaimed during the introductory ceremony at the 2005 Social Venture Institute meetings, which were hosted by SBN. "Business is also a tool for social change." She said, "I know the goat herders who grow the cheese for my restaurant and the farmers from Chiapas who supply my coffee." Before she retired from her restaurant, in 2009, The White Dog Café provided a living wage for all its employees, featured a cruelty-free menu, and used 100 percent wind energy. (The White Dog was the first business in Philadelphia and one of the first in the nation to be totally powered by wind.) Wicks's store became a model for sustainable business both locally and nationally.[8]

It is not surprising that Joe became a member of the Sustainable Business Network. As social-movement theorists stress, social networks influence whether a person is able to sustain involvement in a social movement. In order to participate in a social movement, the sociologist Roger Gould argues, individuals must (1) be connected to a network of like-minded supporters and (2) believe that their actions can create the change that they view as necessary in the world.[9] For fair traders in Philadelphia, traveling to visit artisans and farmers in developing countries instills the belief that fair trade is a necessary form of social activism that can make a difference in the world (more on this in chapter 3). But equally important, according to Gould, is the network of support provided by, in this case, organizations like the SBN and the Independents Coffee Cooperative. For Joe, the people he met through these two organizations helped reinforce his belief that he was doing the right thing.

Meeting Joe

In the fall of 2004, I began hanging out at a couple of fair-trade coffee shops in Philadelphia. I was interested in understanding how consumers think about the idea of ethical shopping. But I didn't usually spend time in coffee shops. At the time, I didn't drink coffee, and I didn't know anyone in Philadelphia's coffee community. Soon after entering Joe's coffee shop, I noticed that the store was filled with pamphlets promoting John Kerry, the Democratic candidate in the upcoming 2004 presidential election. As election day neared, I stopped in the store more often and continued to hear Joe, the store's owner, advocate for Kerry. Joe even carried products that attacked President George W. Bush, like his "Embarrassmints" and "Impeachmints," both with pictures of Bush on the cover of the tin case. Most customers did not seem to mind that Joe supported Kerry, but a handful were clearly frustrated.[10]

On election night, the results of the voting were too close to call. It looked like George Bush was going to win, but Kerry had not conceded. The next morning, with the outcome of the election still in limbo, I returned to Center City. Since the great majority of Philadelphians had voted for Kerry, the mood downtown seemed glum. I stopped into Joe's shop, knowing that with all the political activity in the café, many would be talking about the election. While I was there, Kathleen, my wife, called to say that Kerry had officially withdrawn. He had just called Bush to congratulate him. Immediately after receiving the call, I went to the counter to order another iced tea, and I told Joe about Kerry's decision. Previously, I had greeted Joe only with formalities. We had not yet had a full conversation, and I was uncertain about whether he even recognized me. We talked briefly about how "down" everyone in the city looked. Trying to lighten the mood, Joe proposed a campaign slogan to promote Bush's final term in office: "If you loved Vietnam, you are *really* going to love the next four years." Sick joke, I thought, but funny. At this point, I realized that Joe would remember me the next time I came in the store.[11]

I returned to the café a few days later. After about ninety minutes, I got up to order a second iced tea, and Joe asked me, "How are you holding up this week?" I initially was going to give him the typical Philly response, "Good, how *you* doin'?" But I realized he was referring to the election. I entered into a fifteen-minute conversation with Joe and another regular customer, an art-history doctoral student with brown, curly hair. We talked about the election and the future of the antiwar movement. Joe told quite a few sarcastic jokes. He kept arguing that facts don't matter in politics and that he wanted the United States to be annexed by Canada. Joe talked excitedly about the falsity of ideas such as "freedom" and "democracy." He discussed the absurdity of naming NASA's Mars rovers after these concepts. He also joked about a recent time when he had voiced these opinions among friends and caused the entire room to become silent. Joe struck me as charismatic and smart but not exactly a linear thinker. I blamed it on the caffeine. When we concluded the conversation, I told him about my fair-trade project, and he eagerly agreed to an interview.

I would later learn the significance of gaining Joe's trust. With time, he introduced me to many of the most important entrepreneurs and activists in the city. Many fair-trade supporters agreed to speak with me in large part because they knew that Joe trusted me. Given my friendship with Joe, as well as my obligations as an ethnographer reporting on what I'm actually seeing, I sent a draft of this chapter to Joe for his feedback. His comments (both positive and negative) are found throughout the footnotes of this chapter.

Economic Struggles: September 11, a Shuttered Theater, and Increased Competition

Joe signed his lease for the first fair-trade coffee shop in Philadelphia on September 10, 2001. This was an ominous sign; as Joe jokes, "Things went downhill from there." By 2006, he even began telling customers, "We are a 'for-profit' shop without the profits." That year, he netted only $5,000, and his close friends, business associates, and even an ethnographer studying fair trade in Philadelphia (me!) all recommended that he alter his business plan. But Joe had no intention of closing his café. He took out a line of credit on his home and kept his sinking store afloat until May 2009.

Although Joe signed his lease in September 2001, he officially opened the doors of his café in March 2002. As America entered the early stages of the "War on Terror," the economy was sluggish. Unemployment averaged 4 percent in 2000 but hovered around 6 percent by 2003.[12] Although President Bush encouraged Americans to continue spending to stimulate the economy, many could not or simply did not heed his call. Joe believes the economic downturn hurt the chances for his store to succeed.

To make matters worse, the Forrest Theater, which was located next door to Joe Coffee Bar, announced that it was temporarily closing. The theater underwent renovations during this time and eventually re-opened in 2007 with a significantly reduced schedule. In the past, it had held six to eight performances per week, attracting patrons for evening shows and weekend matinees. Between nine and twelve different shows would come to the Forrest Theater throughout the year. Joe designed his business plan to take advantage of the heavy foot traffic stemming from the theater. The theater complemented Joe's shop perfectly, as theatergoers frequented the café during afternoon and evening hours, when business tended to be slower. Joe estimates that he made between $100 and $200 in profits each time the theater put on a show. Thus, the theater's closing had a huge impact on the viability of his café.

Joe also did not foresee the increased competition he would face from a growing number of café owners. A Belgian-style coffee house and three Starbucks stores all opened within two blocks of his shop. (Joe's involvement with Starbucks is discussed in more depth in chapter 5.) There was already a Cosi restaurant, which sells coffee, and a few independently owned cafés within a couple of blocks of the store. The opening of each new coffee shop had a noticeable impact on the traffic inside Joe's café. Additionally, a bridal shop on Joe's block closed after he opened and was replaced by a fast-food chain, thus eliminating more potential customers. The stagnant post-9/11 economy, the closing of the nearby theater, and increased competition all greatly influenced the viability of the store. Nevertheless, if Joe had made certain decisions differently, he could have improved the chances of his store's success.

Controllable Factors: Business Acumen and Store Aesthetics

"I know how much you paid for those," Cindy yelled to Joe while setting up to sell products for a fair-trade event during poverty awareness week at a local university.

In a calmer voice, Cindy turned to me and explained that she buys the same brand of fair-trade nuts for her store, and "at this price point, there is no way he can turn a profit." Cindy was right, and Joe knew it.

A group of undergraduates at Saint Joseph's University had asked Cindy and Joe to come and talk about their experiences with fair trade.[13] Joe asked me to accompany him and help sell coffee, tea, chocolate, and nuts. Joe was routinely asked to speak at and/or sell products at similar events throughout the city. He gave presentations or sold fair-trade products for the Philadelphia Photographic Society, Chestnut Hill College, Saint Joseph's University, and Green Fest on South Street, and he regularly worked at farmers markets around the city. Cindy, as a co-owner of another fair-trade café, tended to work at similar events. Whereas Joe's knowledge about fair trade is incredibly extensive, Cindy's knowledge about how to run a successful business is equally impressive. Prior to opening her coffee shop, she worked in what she referred to as "corporate America" for a small start-up company. Cindy, although admiring Joe, was greatly annoyed at his pricing of these nuts. Although many years his junior, she was trying to convince Joe, as she had done many times in the past, to pay more attention to the economics of his business. She feared that he would be unable to stay open if he continued down his current path.

When Joe's store first opened, in March 2002, foot traffic was much lower than he expected. His store, although on a heavily trafficked corner in Center City, was set back away from the street, and people often passed by without knowing the café was open. To counter this problem, Joe put a large mannequin in the front of the store. The goal was to make the mannequin look like a customer and convince potential customers that this was a hip café, open for business. And it worked. A couple customers came into the store saying they thought the mannequin was a real person. Others just thought the mannequin was cool and wanted to check out the café. The mannequin became a mainstay in the center of the store. Some customers even dressed it in different T-shirts promoting social causes. It was a creative way for Joe to attract attention to the store. But, unfortunately, the longer the café stayed open, the less time Joe invested in creating savvy marketing campaigns to attract traffic.

In December 2005, Joe was again stressing about the future of his store. Occasionally, he took out his frustrations on his employees. He was never hostile, but he was sarcastic and passive-aggressive. He felt that his younger employees didn't want to work hard, but they wanted to be highly paid and constantly praised. After Joe complained to me that his employees lacked motivation and were not following his directions, I overheard him start this conversation with an employee in his late teens:

"Did you see the episode of *South Park* about the underwear gnomes?"

"The what?"

"The underwear gnomes. They live by the same motto as my employees: (1) Steal underwear, (2) Not yet decided, (3) Become rich and powerful [*laughs*]. I want all my employees to watch this episode."

"Present company excluded," the young barista chuckled.

"Yeah, I guess," Joe mumbled while looking frustrated that his point was not made more clearly.

Joe struggled at times to get his employees to finish their tasks the way he wanted them completed. Eventually, he improved the way he managed his staff. He hired a full-time store manager who was reliable, competent, and friendly. The previous two store managers did not last long and did not get along well with the other employees. This last manager shielded Joe from some of his previous day-to-day frustrations.

By mid-2006, with his store manager firmly in place, Joe stepped up his efforts to bring in more revenue. He knew he couldn't continue down his current path, and he had to decide whether he was going to renew his lease for another five years. He eventually decided to invest in a coffee cart so that he could sell his fair-trade coffee in a kiosk at a new, environmentally friendly building-supply store in Old City called Greenable. He spent $7,000 on a custom-made coffee cart that had been used for only two days in a New York City hotel. Because of a labor conflict with the union in the hotel, management decided not to use the cart and agreed to sell it for less than it had cost. The logic seemed sound: buy the kiosk and pay an employee to staff it full-time during the week. Foot traffic in Old City is relatively high, and the costs (other than labor) of running the cart were minimal. Further, Joe was already selling coffee at a nearby farmers market on Sunday afternoons. Many of his regular customers at the market told him they looked forward to buying coffee from him during the week. The potential payout seemed great.

But Joe's original deal with Greenable fell through. He ran into problems obtaining permits from the city of Philadelphia and then became distracted by a request from the Internal Revenue Service for information about his back taxes. A few months after buying the cart, Joe seemed to realize that he did not have the energy or will to get the kiosk up and running anytime soon. I saw him looking remorsefully at the kiosk and overheard him say to a fellow employee, "I couldn't have shot myself worse in the foot if I had tried."

With no place to store the kiosk, he brought it back to his café, where it sat cluttering the entrance. During the last year that the store was open, the kiosk was often filled with products Joe was trying to sell —knickknacks, coffeemakers, coffee cups, and even books. The initial proceeds from these sales went to fund a Peruvian solar drying project that would allow farmers to improve coffee quality by reducing the beans' exposure to moisture. But the damage done to the aesthetics of the store was significant. As J. M., a customer and self-proclaimed coffee critic on the website Yelp, wrote about the design of the store:

> Unfortunately, the indoor experience is not good. The space is awkward with two entrances (often blowing arctic air in winter months), and the seats, well, they don't inspire long conversations. Plus, the entrance is framed by Joe's ongoing garage sale of unwanted books and junk. I wouldn't describe Joe's as broke but it does need some fixing!

Along these same lines, Joe never seemed to realize the importance of having a clean, baby-friendly bathroom in his store. When the café first opened, Joe had two bathrooms. But, as he negotiated the price of his lease downward, he gave up one of the bathrooms, forcing him to use the remaining one as a storage closet. As the door to the bathroom was opened, the first thing customers saw was an industrial sink, a mop, a large yellow bucket, and cleaning supplies. The bathroom was clean, but I never found it to be as clean as the bathrooms at Starbucks or other independently owned coffee shops in Philadelphia. Perhaps more important, the bathroom did not have a changing table, so the shop was not a desirable location for parents of young children to hang out. Many other cafés in the Independents Coffee Cooperative attracted a large number of parents with their children in the late-morning hours. I rarely saw these customers at Joe's.[14]

Joe is one of the hardest-working coffee entrepreneurs that I observed in Philadelphia. (Hang out with any coffee-shop owner, and you will soon realize how much work goes into making a small business run effectively.) He remained in business for more than seven years, but he never made more than $10,000 a year while owning the café. He often complained about not being able to afford new socks, let alone health insurance. And he took out a large home equity loan to keep his store open. This raises the question why Joe didn't close his café earlier.

Joe's Alternative Reward: A Reputation as an Ethical Entrepreneur

About a year after opening, Joe was becoming frustrated. He was not meeting the financial goals he had established in his business plan, and he was fearful about the future of his café. He told me how he expressed his frustration to Jada, a representative from his coffee supplier at Equal Exchange:

> She was telling me, "Well, your sales are going up. You're doing the right thing. You just have to hang in there." And she told me—and I forget, but roughly she was figuring out what my annual consumption of coffee was. I guess I was open maybe about a year, just shy of a year, a little bit more than a year. And she said that I'm basically selling enough coffee to support almost two farms. It's collectively; it's from all of these different farms all over the world. But collectively, it's enough that two average fair-trade coffee farms employing twenty or thirty people each are being supported by me. And I'm probably doing about three or four coffee farms now [2005], which is a great feeling. I've changed the lives of about one hundred people. And I don't even know where. They have health care and I don't. . . . These people have nothing. And collectively, everybody here . . . has changed a lot of people's lives. That's really a great feeling.

Whereas Joe's financial outlook should have encouraged him to close his café, the positive feelings he derived from helping far-off coffee farmers motivated him to stay in business. Scholars of social movements and collective action refer to this process as an "alternative reward structure." Alternative rewards are the noneconomic processes that encourage individuals to participate in collective action.[15] In the case of fair trade, mission-driven (as opposed to profit-motivated) entrepreneurs receive an emotional high knowing that they are helping to improve the lives of impoverished farmers and artisans. The stories these entrepreneurs tell about where their coffee and handicrafts come from serve to motivate their support for fair-trade initiatives.

Aside from his trip to Italy, the first major high Joe received as a coffee-shop owner came from a trip to Puerto Rico to visit coffee farmers in the summer of 2004. He never intended to meet the farmers who grew his coffee. But, while attending a coffee trade show, he saw that employees of Café Rico, one of his smaller suppliers, had a booth at the show. As he walked by, one of the representatives called out:

> "Would you like to try some Puerto Rican coffee?"
> I gave a little smart remark back, like, "I know how good it is already because I sell it."
> "You sell it? You sell our coffee?"
> "Yeah, I sell your coffee."
> "You're kidding. Where are you from?"
> "Philadelphia."
> "I didn't think we had a place in Philadelphia."
> I said, "You do. You have one. It's me."
> "Oh, come to us."
> "Thank you," Joe said. "If you look to see how much I buy, I don't think you'd be inviting me."
> "Oh yeah. Yeah. It doesn't matter. You come to Puerto Rico; let us know ahead of time. It'll take a whole day. We'll arrange everything."
> And so Joe said to himself, "Maybe I will. Should I?" I just felt stupid. It's like, I don't buy one hundred pounds a year.

The whole interaction made Joe feel like a big-time investor. But Joe's decision to follow up on the offer of a visit had an even more profound impact on him.

The vice president of the company, a marketing director, and a younger man working as a coffee cupper picked Joe up at six in the morning from his bed and breakfast in San Juan. Joe elatedly described one of his first interactions on the trip:

> I loved it. A few minutes into the car [ride], forty-five minutes, and something political came up, gently political. Like if you like to nudge people like I do. It came up. I saw a little wedge. [And I said] . . . , "I

have a feeling you and I have the same politics." I said, "I may be wrong, but I don't support the president. And I think we're fighting a war in the wrong place." That was it. Forty-five minutes into it. [After that], this guy would tell you about anything. He told me about how the U.S. got Puerto Rico because they were liberating Puerto Rico from the Spanish. They didn't invite them in. They just seemed to be still holding on to it. And they talked about the economic problems. And driving around, it was one of the greatest moments in my life. It really was.

"That conversation?" I interrupted.

"The whole thing. The whole day and everything involved. I mean . . . we're driving—there's something—tamarindo. They look like giant green beans, but they're brown, hanging from trees. And we pulled over, and this kid Carlos is climbing up the fence to get onto a tree because the ones that were close weren't good. And him and the other guy are outside. And [I said], "He's going to get shot in the ass."

And he said, "Why? Why?"

"He's climbing on the fence to get high in the tree." I said, "I feel horrible."

"Oh, don't worry. He's fine. If someone comes out—I don't think anyone will come out, but if they do, we'll just tell them you're from the States and what's going on. They'll be okay."

More than anything else, this trip taught Joe how labor-intensive coffee farming can be. His fondest memories involved picking tamarindos alongside the road with his hosts, walking along steep mountain slopes to see shade-grown coffee, and talking politics with his hosts from Café Rico. He explained, "I loved meeting people. I loved finding out about their culture. I wanted them to tell me or show me how they live. I wanted to just see their typical day. I loved that."

A few years later, in January 2006, Joe was selected by his other coffee distributor, Equal Exchange, to travel with a delegation of café owners to Nicaragua. Each year, Equal Exchange pays for some of its buyers to fly abroad and meet with fair-trade farmers. Undoubtedly, the organization is aware that these trips foster greater commitment (alternative rewards) to fair trade and Equal Exchange. The trip came at the perfect time for Joe. He was feeling run-down, not sleeping, and trying to decide whether he should renew the lease for his store. In the weeks leading up to the trip, Joe was increasingly depressed. Far from the infectiously charismatic person I had known for the last few years, Joe now more closely resembled *Saturday Night Live*'s fictional character from the same time period, Debbie Downer. He hoped an eight-day trip to the Nicaraguan *campo* would help him clear his mind and set goals for his future.[16]

Just as he had hoped, Joe came back renewed. He got to use his broken Spanish while playing with local children. Along with his fellow travelers, Joe even met the mayor of one of the towns he visited. (Joe proudly told me the mayor still has a photo of his group in his office. Another traveler on an Equal Exchange tour saw the photo a few years later.) He got a huge rush from meeting with "his" coffee farmers and living alongside fellow fair-trade entrepreneurs. Joe described one of these interactions as especially transformative.

Jada was the only person on the trip to Nicaragua who knew about the struggles Joe was facing with his store. Joe had confided in her when the store first opened. Toward the end of the trip, Jada, Joe, and a few other travelers started talking about what they would do when they returned home. Joe admitted that he had no idea what he was going to do. He told them, "I don't know if my store is going to make it." He went on to reveal some of his hardships and doubts about the future.

The more he went on about himself, the more he felt that he was simply complaining. He told me that the conversation made him feel "incredibly selfish." He saw the living conditions of farmers in Nicaragua and asked himself, "What am I complaining about?" Joe later told me, "I know that I am helping people . . . and [that trip made me realize] that I should not take the things that I have for granted." Joe returned from his trip in better spirits. He was more accepting of his economic struggles and felt that he was willing to accept a lower standard of living. Joe was especially excited to tell customers about his experiences traveling in Nicaragua. But these interactions soon left him frustrated.

In the weeks following the trip, I sat in Joe's shop and heard him talk about Nicaragua. Many customers looked confused, asking Joe why he had chosen to travel there in the first place. While talking about our recent trips to Nicaragua, Joe told me that "the majority of people couldn't grasp the depths of poverty or empathize" with the farmers. One customer, dressed in a white coat from his job at the nearby hospital, simply responded, "To each his own." Another interaction, which Joe later told me about, involved a doctor who was a regular at his café. The doctor was excited to hear about Joe's trip and recounted a story of his own in which he traveled to an exclusive Nicaraguan beachside resort with his wife. This story frustrated Joe, who prefers to have "real experiences with local people." He thought, "You get to learn more about your wife, but you already know your wife . . . [so] what good is that?"

As time passed, Joe talked less and less about his time in Nicaragua. His customers seemed to understand the purpose of his trip to Puerto Rico, as some had been there and most had at least some knowledge about the island. But few people knew much about Nicaragua. Those who were able to converse about the country really caught Joe's attention. At least a couple times a week, people came into the café because they knew Joe had been to Nicaragua, they had heard about Joe's work in fair trade, they wanted to open a fair-trade business, or they wanted to talk about their future plans to work in a nonprofit organization. Local college professors sent their students to Joe's shop to learn about fair trade, organic issues, and antisweatshop initiatives. Two art-school professors publicized a green map of the city inside the store, and the café was even featured on the front page of a prominent Dutch newspaper. Joe Café was later voted one of the top ten green companies in America by Co-Op America. This final nomination culminated in a local leadership award from Co-Op America (now Green America), which was especially impressive. The great majority of the other nominees for the top green business were chain stores with multiple locations around the country. Voting required customers to visit the Green America website and vote. The contest showed that, although Joe did not have a large customer base, those who did support him were very loyal.

But most of these experiences did not draw significant numbers of new customers to the café. The emotional high Joe received from his prominent status within the ethical-consumption community did not pay off with the economic rewards required to keep him in business.

Closing Shop—the Tax Man Cometh

In July 2008, Joe learned he was being audited by the Internal Revenue Service. The agency had looked over his finances and come to the conclusion that something was amiss. From a purely economic viewpoint, the only viewpoint from which the IRS is supposed to be making decisions, Joe's café did not make sense. His profits were minimal and likely raised some suspicions among auditors. At the time, Joe was frustrated, but he understood their concerns. He met with his accountant and began putting together his paperwork. In hindsight, Joe told me in the fall of 2011, he should have gotten a lawyer. A friend from the Sustainable Business Network recommended that he do this when she learned of the audit, telling him, "You have no idea what you are up against."

The phone calls, meetings, and requests from the IRS for more paperwork did not cease. Joe, already at his wits' end and knowing, on some level, that his store was going to have to close, was becoming frustrated. The frustration began to turn to anger. Facing bankruptcy and struggling to make one last-ditch effort to keep his store alive, he had no extra time to devote to the audit. Whereas all the other founding members of the Independents Coffee Cooperative co-owned their coffee shops, Joe was alone. He simply did not have sufficient time to deal with the audit and run his store.

By late October 2008, Joe was really losing it. I entered his store at 8:30 one morning hoping to sit in on a meeting with him, his accountant, and two members of the IRS. Joe told me he wanted me present as a "witness to their nonsense." Joe had not slept at all the night before. He was nervous about the meeting and wanted to make sure he had all his paperwork in order so that he could "get back to running [his] business." The meeting was scheduled for 9:00 in the office of Joe's accountant. At 8:45, minutes before we were to leave for the meeting, Joe received a call from his accountant saying that it had been canceled.

"Ask her [the auditor] if she wants me to close the store," Joe screamed into the phone for everyone in the café to hear. "Ask her if she wants me to close the store while I go out and find the information she needs."

Joe's accountant had sent all the documents that the IRS requested through FedEx two weeks prior to the meeting. The agents had looked over the material and called that morning to say they would not be coming out. They also informed Joe that they wanted to open a new account for 2007, and they wanted more bank statements. After learning of this, Joe called the auditor. Barely able to contain himself, he exclaimed, "What am I supposed to do with the extra staff that I put on for the day? This is inappropriate!" He had to pay for both an extra employee to staff the store and his accountant, who had cleared his schedule for the morning. After a long pause, he ended the call by asking for her "supervisor's phone number."

About ten minutes later, he got the supervisor on the phone and explained his situation. With a flushed red face, Joe talked loudly into the phone. At this time, eight customers were in the store. "I don't know anyone who doesn't think this is absurd. You want more bank statements, you got them. [Sarcastically] When would you like them? I'm just glad I have extra employees to hear everything that is going on. Are you forwarding all of this to Senator [Arlen] Specter's office? Specter's office has been involved with this since the third month [of the audit]."

After hanging up the phone, Joe stepped away from the register and into the back of the shop. Around this same time, a young medical student approached the counter. I had not seen her in the store previously. She quietly said to the barista, "This coffee is cold. Do you have a microwave back there?"

As Joe plowed more and more of his resources into dealing with his audit, his business suffered. (This is not to suggest that he would have survived without the audit, as I do not believe that would have been the case.) He spent $7,000 on a coffee cart that ended up being used as a fold-out table at the front of the store. But he also lost the potential revenue that he would have gained by making the cart operational. He removed himself more and more from the day-to-day operations of the store. As he dealt with the auditors, customers complained about cold coffee and the store's poor aesthetics. It was an incredibly frustrating time for Joe. He wrote angry letters to the local media, the mayor, members of Congress, and even President Barack Obama. In these letters, he stressed that he was a "small business owner," the founder of the first "fair trade coffee house in Philadelphia," and a retailer of "local foods from family farms." It seemed he was holding out hope that his work as an ethical entrepreneur would help him with the audit.

At no point did I doubt the veracity of Joe's bank statements or finances. I knew that he had holes in many of his socks, I knew he wore his jeans until they began to fall apart, I knew how much he worked, I knew he did not have health insurance, I knew he did not have the business acumen of some his colleagues, and I knew that the foot traffic in his store was nowhere near that of many of the other Independents shops. Nevertheless, without inside access to all of Joe's records, it was a little unclear to me how the IRS was going to weigh in on the audit.

When the dust settled, Joe was found to owe $1,571 for his 2006 federal taxes and $394 for his 2007 federal taxes. The auditor, who said she "knows [Joe] has money," never uncovered any major financial problems. But the audit itself devastated Joe financially and emotionally. He owed more than $10,000 to his accountant for all the extra time he had spent preparing for the meetings with the IRS. His retirement funds were depleted, and he no longer had any equity left in his home. Joe knew he would soon have to file for bankruptcy. Increasingly, he began to accept the notion that the first fair-trade café in Philadelphia was going to close.

Conclusion: "For Profit, without the Profit"

All business owners make decisions on a daily basis that put their moral ideals and their financial status in conflict with each other. But, given the importance of moral reputations, there is more at stake in these decisions for entrepreneurs who are selling products advertised as ethical than for other business owners.[17] If a manager at Ten Thousand Villages or the owner of an Independents café were to be seen shopping at Walmart, for instance, her reputation could suffer greatly. In this Twitter- and Facebook-dominated age, feedback on a moral gaffe is quick and potentially damaging. Restaurant reviews are immediately posted on websites like Yelp, enabling anecdotal experiences to become viewed as objective realities. As a result, store owners spend a lot of time deciding how important green, fair-trade, organic, and sustainable initiatives are for their moral reputations. One Independents café owner captures this tension between moral ideals and profitability perfectly when e-mailing Joe and the other Independents owners about which coffee cups to purchase:

I suspect that if compostable cups go to the landfill it's not much different than plastic cups sitting in the landfill. I don't think the corn cups are
recyclable. . . . I wonder if producing cups from corn rather than petro-
leum is superior for the environment or if it takes less energy. . . . Geez,
trying to do the right thing starts to get a little complicated, eh? I guess
we have to decide if it's worth an extra $5/case and the hassle of switch-
ing suppliers.

Store owners like Joe are confronted with these options on a daily basis.
They need to figure out whether customers will criticize them as hypocritical for the types of cups they provide or the brand of coffee they
sell. They want to run a profitable business, but it takes a lot of work to
maintain a niche as an ethical entrepreneur.[18]

In this chapter, I have sought to describe Joe's experiences in the fair-
trade marketplace. His story illustrates some of the tensions and meaningful moments in his quest to maintain both his moral reputation and
a profitable business. His devotion to fair trade and other social-justice
initiatives inspired a small but loyal following of customers. Joe's customers and other conscientious consumers from throughout Philadelphia are the focus of chapters 4 and 5. The next chapter takes a broader
approach in examining the experiences that have encouraged many
consumers and fair-trade entrepreneurs to become promoters and to
commit themselves to living a fair-trade life.

3

"Buy More Coffee"

Becoming a Promoter through Extraordinary Experiences

Soon after booking my "reality tour" to a fair-trade coffee coopera-tive in Nicaragua, I learned that in 1972, Roberto Clemente's plane had crashed on his way to this same Central American country. Clemente was a perennial all-star in Major League Baseball who was known for his humanitarian work throughout Latin America. My mind turned to the other snippets of information I knew about Nicaragua: the coffee crisis, the Contra war, and the country's status as the second poorest in the western hemisphere. While not a fatalist at heart, I could not ignore the fact that almost all the knowledge I possessed about Nicaragua was tragic. I later learned that those who travel to live with coffee farmers tend to return home telling similarly tragic stories. These travelers do not talk about extravagant vacations and luxurious accommodations. They describe the poor living conditions they experienced during their visits to the *campo* (countryside). They talk about the lack of electric-ity, the slow pace of life, the ever-present poverty, and the impact of war. I was not immune; I told family and friends about my innumerable flea bites, upset stomachs, dirty outhouses, and delicious but unchanging meals of *gallopinto* (rice and beans). With time, I came to realize the importance of these stories. Through the telling and retelling of these experiences, individuals feel part of the fair-trade movement and become increasingly motivated to seek out ethical products.

This chapter looks at the ways face-to-face interactions with farmers and artisans help motivate activists to support fair trade. These activists, whom I refer to as "promoters," organize informational campaigns describing what fair trade means, open their own mission-driven businesses to help artisans and farmers, and closely align their altruistic values with their everyday purchases as consumers. Joe Cesa, discussed in the previous chapter, is just one example of a fair-trade promoter. Many of the altruistic actions guiding promoters stem from the belief that fair trade can improve people's lives. This belief is instilled within promoters through the stories that fair-trade farmers and artisans share with them.

The chapter begins by defining and explaining the importance of "extraordinary experiences." These emotionally intense trips to far-off developing countries serve as a tipping point for many promoters, leading them to a life of activism. The second half of the chapter describes situations in which artisans and farmers are paraded around the United States. Sponsored by large fair-trade importers, artisans and farmers travel throughout the country telling stories about how fair trade helped improve their communities. While not as emotionally intense as travel abroad, these presentations are designed to promote widespread support of fair trade. I explain that many of these presentations are remarkably effective, but others fail to generate long-term support for fair trade.

The Significance of Extraordinary Experiences

Behavioral psychologists, sociologists, and marketers have shown that emotions can influence our judgments, affect our behavior, and alter the way we think about past experiences.[1] Daniel Kahneman, winner of the Nobel Prize in economics, writes, "The world in our heads is not a precise replica of reality; our expectations about the frequency of events are distorted by the prevalence and emotional intensity of the messages to which we are exposed."[2] Whereas Kahneman's work shows how emotions shape our judgments, the sociologist Randall Collins explains that behavior is greatly motivated by our conscious and unconscious desire to seek out positive emotional energy. Collins emphasizes the importance of positive "interaction rituals" that create a sense of elation, enthusiasm, and a desire to take initiative. When we experience fulfilling social interactions, the resulting emotional energy motivates us to seek out similarly rewarding interactions. Thus, our actions are chained together by a desire to seek out emotional energy.[3]

Eric Arnould and Linda Price, both professors of marketing, describe emotionally intense, "magical," and "transformative" events as "extraordinary experiences."[4] These experiences are characterized by immersion into a new social context or place, a sense of "joy and valuing," a "spontaneous letting-be of the process, and a newness of perception and process." Extraordinary experiences are "unusual events" that are often triggered by face-to-face interactions. Participants recall their experiences fondly, but, because of their intense emotional feelings, they often have a difficult time describing the story to outsiders.

Within the world of fair trade, the opportunity to live and work alongside an impoverished coffee farmer in Nicaragua, a basket weaver in Bangladesh, or a Tuareg silversmith in Niger are examples of extraordinary experiences. Such travels have encouraged many promoters to more fully invest in a purpose-driven life. The trips instill a belief that fair trade and socially responsible products can make a significant difference in poor people's lives.[5]

As soon as I started speaking with promoters in the fair-trade movement, I began hearing stories about the importance of international travel. Most said that travel to developing countries either sparked their interest or greatly motivated their continued support for fair trade. Stacey, a woman in her mid-twenties from Scotland who twice traveled to Central America, explained that interacting with fair-trade coffee farmers in Nicaragua "produced enthusiasm" for fair trade among her fellow travelers. Ashley, referring to a trip to Mexico, went so far as to say that she "would not be the same person" if she had not seen for herself how local workers struggled to survive. International travelers cited dinners with host families, interactions with farmers and artisans, and conversations with local activists as having the most profound impact on their views of fair trade.

David and Jennifer told me that their lives changed significantly after they decided to go backpacking throughout Southeast Asia. They met in high school, and David asked Jennifer out on a date, but she kept telling him "no." Over time, as David jokes, she "broke down and agreed to go out with me." While in college, David and Jennifer grew closer and eventually married. They got jobs after college, but were not entirely sure what they were going to do for their careers. They both had traveled extensively before embarking on a backpacking tour of Southeast Asia. David explained, "I [had] been to Canada. . . . I [had] been to Greece and Italy, but that was on our honeymoon" and "only for two weeks." David told me that those trips "gave me the taste" for international travel. He enjoyed them, but he does not view them as transformative like his trip with Jennifer to Indonesia, Malaysia, Thailand, Cambodia, Vietnam, Singapore, Laos, and Hong Kong. This latter trip "was a catalyst for the [fair-trade] coffee shop . . . seeing how life is more about interacting and having fun and kicking back." He continued, "There's a lot of people we ran into that worked eighteen-hour days, but they were having fun while they were doing it."

Dave and Jennifer were in a small fishing village in Indonesia during the terrorist attacks of September 11, 2001. As they pondered the next steps in their life together, they relished the sense of community found in the coffee shops they visited. Writing on their store's website, they explained, "Perhaps it was a splintering global community, perhaps it was the warm fuzzy feeling [we] got when [we] thought about the people and places that awaited [us upon our return home]. Whatever it was, a coffee shop where neighbors met and engaged with one another and with members of the world coffee community began to take shape in those hills." For David and Jennifer, the trip to Southeast Asia enhanced their belief that they are part of a global community. Their store is guided by a "sense of local and global community." Their menu is filled with organic, local, and fair-trade items. And as David told me during our interview, the impetus for the store came from their experiences in Southeast Asia: "It was a life-changing trip. Absolutely. Absolutely."

Talking with other local and national fair-trade activists, I heard countless stories like that of David and Jennifer. Abigail, for instance, got her master's degree in journalism before deciding to travel across Central America. She said that traveling throughout Central America "opened [my] eyes," and she decided to move to El Salvador. Working closely with "small-scale coffee farmers" allowed Abigail to "see their troubles" and to better understand the issues surrounding development in third-world countries. Her vacation destination eventually became her home of nine years. During her time in Central America, she kept wrestling with the notion of "how hard coffee farmers have it and how the system is set up against them." In essence, her carefree travel experiences throughout Central America led her to a life advocating for fair trade. She now works for a large fair-trade importing company. Her trips made her believe that she is part of a global coffee community. Moreover, she told me that "we live in a disempowered society where it is difficult to hear your voice in political channels." For this reason, she believes it is important to treat our everyday purchases as a form of political action. Her experiences along the coffee supply chain convinced her that fair trade can improve farmers' lives.

Whereas Abigail, Jennifer, David, and many other fair-trade promoters traveled to developing countries on their own initiative, many others were sent to live with artisans and farmers by a large fair-trade importing company. Each year, Equal Exchange, the importer that provides the majority of the coffee for the Independents cafés in this study, and Ten Thousand Villages attempt to create extraordinary experiences for their store managers and owners by organizing trips to meet with fair-trade farmers and artisans. These trips provide a shared experience for small groups of fair-trade promoters; they learn about fair-trade standards, meet with fair-trade producers, and live in their communities. Upper-level managers at Ten Thousand Villages told me that these trips foster a "deeper commitment" to the organization and to the fair-trade mission. Upon returning home, managers are able to sell the products they saw being made at a much higher rate than before the trip.[6]

Jocelyn, a Ten Thousand Villages store manager, returned from a Ten Thousand Villages–funded trip to India and Bangladesh with a renewed commitment to helping fair-trade artisans. Prior to the trip, she sold products from India and Bangladesh by telling stories that she learned from the company website and at Ten Thousand Villages training sessions. But, after her travels, those stories came alive. She wanted to relay the significance of her trip to the volunteers in the store. So she spent almost two hours giving a slideshow presentation that included more than 145 pictures from her trip. One of the most dramatic images contrasts the hotel where the volunteers stayed in India with the slums located just outside the hotel's boundary. Other pictures showed close-up views of people's faces, primarily those of women and children. Jocelyn described how the artisans she met in Bangladesh produce greeting cards by cutting pieces of straw and gluing them by hand onto colorful pieces of paper. She said that "the process takes two to three hours, and the cards only retail for about $3 in the store." She also created a scrapbook with pictures showing each stage in the process of producing the greeting cards. Every picture in Jocelyn's slideshow included a caption describing the ways various products in the store are produced. Her enthusiasm extended to the work she did in the shop: she approached customers about products from India and Bangladesh, she described the labor-intensive processes involved in handicraft production, and she told customers stories about the poor living conditions of the artisans she had met.

Cindy, a co-owner of an Independents café, was dreaming about starting a coffee shop with a friend when she was unexpectedly laid off from her job. She told me, "I kinda took that as an opportunity to regroup and think about what I want to do . . . do I really want to work for this huge company?" She decided that she wanted to "go smaller," and she got a job five blocks from where she lived. The job was still in her area of expertise—Internet technology—but it was "more along the lines of a startup Web development" company. But Cindy still didn't like what she was doing. She was developing sales training material for pharmaceutical companies when she again asked herself, "What am I doing?" Two weeks before getting laid off for a second time, she "happened to be part of a conversation . . . about opening a coffee house." She encouraged her two friends to "just do it!" She offered to help write a business plan to get the store going, but, at the time, she wasn't willing to be a partner in the café. She was worried because her friends knew little about "the financials." She joked, somewhat seriously, "They both had liberal arts degrees in, like, psychology!"

Cindy eventually decided to join her friend Sarah and open the coffee shop. (The third friend opted out of the partnership.) While Cindy was focusing on developing a profitable business, Sarah kept talking about the importance of fair-trade coffee. It was July 2002, and, even within the coffee world, the idea of fair trade was not widely understood. Cindy agreed to sell coffee from the fair-trade importer Equal Exchange but only because it scored very well in blind taste tests. Cindy admitted, however, that she didn't really understand what fair trade meant.

Sarah and Cindy's café became profitable very quickly. It seems Sarah was right in her assessment that "the only thing this neighborhood [was] missing [was] a good coffee house." The store is still in an excellent location. No other coffee shop sits within a three-block radius, and people from outside the neighborhood frequent the store because of a few local tourist attractions. With sales exceeding expectations, their coffee supplier, Equal Exchange, offered Cindy, as well as David, mentioned earlier, the opportunity to travel with a small group of fair-trade store owners to see how coffee is grown in Nicaragua. Cindy explained to me that the trip transformed "my understanding of fair trade and made me much more committed to it."

Upon returning home, Cindy prominently displayed pictures from her trip throughout her store, and she no longer questioned her decision to carry fair-trade coffee. She even hosted a slideshow presentation of her trip at Saint Joseph's University and at her own café. She wanted customers and students to understand how labor-intensive coffee production can be.

I met Cindy for the first time during her Nicaragua presentation at her store. Most of the fifty or so attendees were members of the Sustainable Business Network (SBN). (SBN was, as noted in chapter 1, started by Judy Wicks, the founder of the White Dog Café. Judy and her store have received national acclaim for helping pioneer the notion of a socially responsible restaurant.) As such, most of the audience members were sympathetic to fair trade. They listened intently as the presentation began with a short film emphasizing the benefits of fair trade for coffee farmers in Costa Rica and Nicaragua. The film kept emphasizing that our everyday actions can create change in the "global community."

Cindy focused on how coffee moves from a Nicaraguan farm to a Philadelphia coffee house. She started by proclaiming, "The number one thing I learned about fair trade was the quality issue." As the farmers become more educated about what makes good coffee, more and more "quality control" measures are put into place to ensure that the farmers are getting the best beans onto the market. Further, the fair-trade supply chain is more beneficial to farmers than conventional supply chains because there are fewer people involved in getting the coffee to the United States. In many conventional coffee supply chains, coffee needs to move through ten different steps to get to a café. The farmers grow and pick the coffee, but then, after selling the beans to a "coyote," the farmer receives no more economic benefits as the beans move along the supply chain. (Coyotes, as I explained in chapter 1, are viewed as predatory coffee buyers in Central America. They are thought to have extensive knowledge about the global price of coffee and use that to their advantage when negotiating sales with farmers who know little about the price of coffee in international markets.) In a fair-trade setup, the coffee moves through about six stages before reaching the U.S. market. Farmers are part of "democratically elected cooperatives" that wash, dry, sort, and ship the beans to the United States. These cooperatives reduce the number of steps in the supply chain.[7] This permits the farmers to retain more profit than they would in conventional markets.

Cindy continued her presentation by discussing several complicated issues that few people in the coffee world understand in much depth. She talked about how the fair-trade philosophy helps farmers with "credit and land reform, processing and distribution issues, social programs, organic certification, and income diversification." This last issue is particularly important given the most-recent coffee crisis that originated in 2001. (The oversupply of coffee during this crisis drove down prices and led writers in the *Economist* to label fair trade a "misguided" attempt to help farmers that promotes overproduction and creates inefficiencies.)[8] Some leaders in the fair-trade movement encourage farmers to diversify their crops. During the coffee crisis, small-scale farmers who were growing only coffee were devastated by the collapse in coffee prices. Thus, fair-trade farmers are increasingly persuaded to grow cacao, bananas, and other fruits and vegetables that will be profitable in both local and global markets.[9]

Cindy's breadth and depth of knowledge captivated the audience, and when she finished, a woman in her mid-thirties asked, "What more can we do to help these people?" Cindy was prepared for this question. "I asked this same question to the farmers, and they said straight up, 'Buy more coffee.'" In a neoliberal era in which, wrong or right, markets are increasingly viewed as a more effective means for promoting economic growth than state intervention, the idea that fair trading can reduce global poverty was quite attractive to this audience of socially responsible entrepreneurs.

"Buying more" coffee or handicrafts is a phrase cited throughout the movement by fair-trade artisans, farmers, and advocates. It is a compelling narrative for a number of reasons. It implies that fair trade is not simply a charity; it will not create dependence on economic aid. It implies that the artisans are truly deserving of support; after all, they are working hard to produce these products. And it implies that both producers and consumers will be empowered through fair trade; both will feel that they can change the world through trading within this global community of like-minded altruists. The notion of buying more is viewed as a market-driven, yet "sustainable" means for enhancing economic development. Buying more is a convenient and cheap way for consumers to perform an altruistic deed.

Cindy's trip to Nicaragua greatly enhanced her knowledge of fair trade and increased her commitment to buying and selling other socially responsible products. In many ways, Cindy's travel experience and her presentations afterward are typical of the activities of the promoters I met. The activists with whom I traveled to Nicaragua, for example, returned to the United States to write articles for local and national publication, initiate campaigns to get their supermarkets to carry fair-trade coffee, create blogs to describe their experiences, and present slideshows of their trips at local coffee shops, churches, and schools. Mike, a fellow traveler on my trip to Nicaragua, told me, "If my coworkers thought I talked about fair trade a lot before, wait until I get home." Traveling to see the production of fair-trade products helped motivate the promoters to continue supporting the fair trade movement and bolstered their commitment to a socially conscious belief system.

Parading Producers: Face-to-Face Interactions

Though less intense than the full-immersion experience characteristic of trips sponsored by fair-trade companies, face-to-face interactions with producers in the United States still tend to enhance promoters' support for fair trade. Fair Trade USA, Equal Exchange, Ten Thousand Villages, United Students for Fair Trade and a few other fair-trade

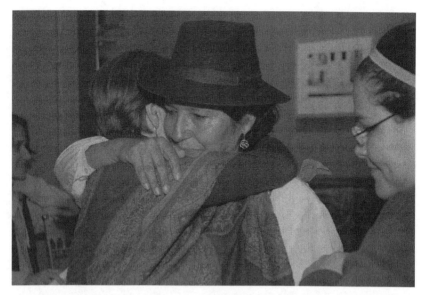

The Independents Coffee Cooperative hosted Eulalia Valdez Palomino (pictured here) and Beltran Leguia Masias, two fair-trade farmers from Peru in the fall of 2007. This photo was taken at Infusion in Mount Airy after Beltran and Eulalia described how fair trade benefits their community. Photo by Pamela Lowe.

organizations routinely bring coffee farmers and handicraft artisans to conferences, retail stores, colleges, and employee workshops in the United States.

At their 2006 spring workshop, Ten Thousand Villages hosted five producers from Guatemala, India, Bangladesh, and Niger. These annual gatherings bring together store managers from across the country to learn more about fair trade. The workshop was held at Lancaster Bible College in central Pennsylvania. The highlight of the meetings is the presentations by the artisans who make a few of the products sold through Ten Thousand Villages. Illies Mouhmoud, a master silversmith from Niger, wearing his traditional blue robe, met with attendees throughout the three days of meetings. Illies is part of a nomadic tribe called the Tuaregs. The Tuaregs traveled across the borders of Burkina Faso, Niger, and a few other African countries before national borders were established, thus ending up widely dispersed among several countries. The Tuaregs tell their history orally, so Illies is not sure when his people began to be split up by the creation of borders. Illies first met a buyer from Ten Thousand Villages while he was traveling in Burkina Faso, and Ten Thousand Villages initially sold his silver jewelry as if it were made in Burkina Faso. It took the organization a while to realize that he actually lived in Niger. They eventually corrected the narratives associated with Illies's jewelry.

After Illies told his story to the entire gathering of store managers, the workshop broke into smaller sessions in which the artisans showed how they make their products. Illies gave a demonstration of how he and his fellow Tuaregs make silver jewelry. He sat cross-legged on the grass outside the chapel at Lancaster Bible College. The other participants, almost all of whom were women, spread out in a circle around him. Some sat on the ground, others stood, and still others sat on chairs. A local news crew filmed the workshop. A few of the women, presumably knowing Illies was coming, were wearing the same style of the jewelry that he was making.

Illies could not get the charcoal hot enough to melt the silver. In Niger, he uses a hard wood that gets much hotter than the "easy-light charcoal" that he was given. He joked that he would be "embarrassed" to tell his friends at home that he could not even melt the silver. Eventually he skipped the melting stage and began molding and shaping the jewelry with sandpaper and a few other tools. While he was working, a woman leaned over to me and whispered, "That is sooo coooool." A store manager flirted with him through the two interpreters who were present. She asked a friend to take a picture of her and Illies. Many others snapped photos throughout the entire presentation.

After the demonstration, Jocelyn, the store manager who had recently traveled to India and Bangladesh, and I began a conversation with Illies and a buyer from Ten Thousand Villages. Jocelyn and Illies knew each other from previous conversations. The buyer had met Illies in Niger and interpreted our conversation. As we talked, people continued to come out of the chapel. One woman, an assistant manager at a new store, came over to listen. The group surrounding Illies quickly grew to include five more people. Within a few minutes, another manager approached and nudged me out of the way to get closer to Illies.

The conversation focused on strategies to make the silver jewelry both less labor-intensive to produce and more cost-effective. One manager suggested eliminating two small circles around the outside of the silver earrings. This would allow the silver to be mixed with nickel, which is significantly cheaper. This strategy would not make the earrings less attractive, but it would make the products cheaper to produce—presumably increasing the economic returns for Illies and his coworkers. The buyer mentioned that the silver is what is "traditionally used by the Tuareg" and that they "aren't very used to mixing the silver." The manager who had moved me out of the way to get closer to Illies was not shy. She emphasized that "we" (referring to herself and Jocelyn—without Jocelyn's consent) thought that the silver "should not be mixed if it is not traditional." The buyer countered that Ten Thousand Villages seeks traditional designs used by the Tuareg people, but, if "it comes down to it," the company wants designs that will sell well in its North American stores. The pushy store manager replied, "We only want the products produced in a traditional manner." She emphasized this point two or three more times before Jocelyn excused us from the conversation by saying, "I should get some coffee."

From my experiences, this was a typical producer-promoter interaction. Promoters fawn over the craftsmanship of the artisans, elevating it to more of an art with comments such as, "Oh, I could never make a product as beautiful as that" and "Can you believe the skill it took to make this?"[10] They circle around the artisan, creating a barrier between those facing the artisan and those outside the group. The promoters take great pride in the authenticity of the artisans' stories. Thus, the idea that an untraditional technique would be used by these artisans becomes a threat to the jewelry's authenticity.[11] The narratives accompanying the jewelry become less compelling if consumers realize that the products were specifically designed to meet their aesthetic preferences. The artisans, for their part, obligingly demonstrate the production process and detail the associated improvements in their livelihoods stemming from fair trade. They become the main attraction for promoters. And, by and large, most artisans (and farmers) are more concerned with improving their economic and social livelihoods than with maintaining some semblance of "tradition."

Once the conference ended, I returned to my weekly volunteer position at Ten Thousand Villages in Philadelphia. During my next shift, I was surprised at how quickly my eyes darted to all the items I had seen produced the previous weekend: the hand-woven jute baskets from India and Bangladesh, the colorful bracelets from Guatemala, the silver jewelry from Niger. Even though I knew that the products in our store were likely made by other artisans, I could not help describing them as Illies's earrings, Suraiya's jute baskets, and Concepcion's hand-woven jewelry.[12]

A few months after the workshop, a white woman in her late thirties entered our store and asked to see the silver earrings prominently displayed near our cash register. This was the first time a customer asked me about a product that I had seen made by Illies, Suraiya, or Concepcion. I was a bit surprised at myself—I became really eager to tell Illies's story. I said, "I recently met Illies, and I saw how he makes these earrings." I told her that Illies lives in a nomadic tribe of Tuaregs near the border of Niger. I described the colorful blue robes that he wore, and I noted the importance of fair trade in his life. The customer listened to my story patiently, then responded that she "knew about Illies from the Ten Thousand Villages website." She "liked the design" of the earrings and was "intrigued" by Illies's story. Although she ended up purchasing the earrings, I felt cheated. Didn't this customer understand that I had actually met Illies? Why didn't she care more about my authentic interaction with Illies? Of course, the joke was on me. I was caring more about status in the fair-trade community than about the economic benefits conveyed to Illies through this purchase.

Meeting Illies seemed to be an effective way of getting store managers and volunteers to tell more detailed and authentic stories about the products they sell. Illies's story was designed to imbue the silver earring with additional value. And, for me, it worked. I excitedly told Illies's story months after I had met him.[13] And, as Jocelyn, our store manager, routinely told the volunteers and employees at her store, the better stories we can tell, the more products we can sell—and, most important, the more people's lives "we" can improve. Interestingly, however, not all interactions with farmers or artisans in the United States lead to a greater motivation to support fair trade.

On a cool October evening in 2006, a representative from Fair Trade USA, David Funkhouser, hosted a Peruvian fair-trade coffee farmer named Cesar Rivas at Joe Coffee Bar in Center City Philadelphia. David works in the public-relations department of Fair Trade USA, the certifying organization that establishes fair-trade standards for food entering the United States. Fair Trade USA played a seminal role in growing the fair-trade market by providing a level of trust to consumers that the product was certified by an independent organization and helped expand the market for farmers by marketing fair-trade coffee.

David and Cesar arrived at Joe Coffee Bar looking exhausted. They were in the midst of traveling throughout the Northeast talking to college students, coffee-shop customers, and church groups. They had given two presentations earlier that day. David acted as both an interpreter and a moderator of the talk. He framed the discussion by highlighting the goals of Fair Trade USA: to improve farmers' lives by increasing the total amount of fair-trade coffee sold. Most of the attendees had little understanding of Fair Trade USA's central role in the movement, and most were unfamiliar with the passionate debates about whether Fair Trade USA is doing enough to help farmers. (At a national level, Fair Trade USA was and continues to be criticized by promoters for its emphasis on increasing the market share of fair-trade products, rather than on improving the social and economic living conditions of farmers. Fair Trade USA believes change will occur only with the support of big corporations such as Starbucks, McDonald's, and even Walmart. Organizations that buy Fair Trade USA–certified coffee in bulk receive a discount on the fair-trade certification. This infuriates small buyers who sell only 100-percent-certified coffees.)

Cesar did not look like the coffee farmers in most of the fair-trade advertisements. Instead of dirty old jeans and a T-shirt, he wore nice leather shoes, khaki pants, and a stylish dress shirt. We learned that this was Cesar's fourth time visiting the United States. Local leaders and cooperative presidents are the most likely farmers to be sent to speak at conferences and stores in the United States. They tend to be the most highly educated members of the cooperatives. In this instance, I wondered how the audience would look at Cesar. I cynically suspected that arriving with a mule like the old Juan Valdez advertisements would have given him a bit more credibility. Cesar described the benefits his cooperative receives by selling fair-trade-certified coffee and then took questions from the audience. It did not take long before the discussion moved to chain stores and Starbucks.

Chris, who identified himself as an employee of Trader Joe's, a chain store selling many fair-trade and organic products, described his frustration with profit-driven companies, saying that he "wants to support fair trade" but that "I don't want to buy it at a chain store like Starbucks." The comment seemed fairly harmless, and most of the fifteen to twenty people in attendance nodded their heads in agreement. Chris went on to justify his own work at a chain store by explaining that Trader Joe's sells "many socially responsible products." David smiled, looking like he had heard this criticism of Starbucks many times before. He then interpreted the comment for Cesar. Cesar responded by saying that his cooperative sells much of its coffee to "small coffee buyers." He then proudly explained that "our cooperative's biggest buyer is Starbucks." David smiled again; he anticipated that this statement was going to frustrate many of those present. The attendees seemed to be at a loss for words. They did not know how to respond. I could almost see the wheels turning in people's heads: "How could this farmer who we support so much want to sell his coffee to Starbucks? Doesn't he have any standards?"

Joe, who also attended the presentation, later told me that he was taken aback by Cesar's comment. Almost all of his coffee was certified as fair trade, while, at the time, only about 5 to 8 percent of Starbucks' coffee was fair trade. Worse yet, Starbucks had opened two new stores within two blocks of his café. One of the stores gave out gift certificates for free coffee to the customers who were sitting in the seats outside his café. Joe was frustrated that Fair Trade USA would promote Starbucks at a fair-trade coffee house.

I suspected that Cesar's comment would deeply affect the people in attendance. I thought this might be a turning point for many of them. Perhaps they would acknowledge that Starbucks plays an important role in the fair-trade movement. Whereas the percentage of Starbucks coffee that is fair-trade-certified may be small, the company is still the largest buyer of fair-trade beans in the United States. I thought that those present would consider the part that Starbucks plays in improving the lives of Peruvian farmers like Cesar. I soon learned that I was completely wrong.

A few days later, while volunteering at Ten Thousand Villages, I asked Jocelyn, the store manager, what she thought about Cesar's presentation. She said she had talked with Betty, a friend who attended the presentation, about the "Starbucks issue," and they both thought it was just a form of "propaganda." They both admitted that it was "probably okay" for Cesar to sell his coffee to Starbucks, but they do not want to support this company. Both Jocelyn and Betty felt "betrayed" that Fair Trade USA would advocate, even if only implicitly, shopping at Starbucks. The women's distrust of Starbucks has built up over a long period of time, and even Cesar's stories could not break their hostility toward this corporation. They feel that Starbucks is solely profit-driven and sells fair-trade coffee only to shield itself from criticism by consumer activists. They are promoters who have a more rigid definition of ethical consumption than many of their customers. They strive to reduce the contradictions between their ideals and their shopping patterns and position themselves as different from conscientious consumers and purchasers who are unable to do this. For both Jocelyn and Betty, Cesar's stories and possibly even his well-dressed appearance were not persuasive enough to get them to purchase fair-trade coffee at a place like Starbucks.

Returning Home from the *Campo*

I kept hearing from promoters how "transformative," "intense," and "life changing" their experiences living with fair-trade farmers and artisans had been. I did not doubt their sincerity. They were not pretending; all the promoters had a deep emotional commitment to fair trade.[14] But I was critical of the notion that you could "see for yourself" how fair trade impacts farmers. As a social scientist, I felt that the only way to understand whether fair trade is actually improving farmers and artisans' lives is by systematically comparing fair trade and nonfair-trade communities over time. But there are currently very few empirically sound studies that are able to compare these types of communities. Some preliminary findings show that fair trade provides improved economic, health, and educational outcomes for farming families in Central America.[15] Other research implies that fair trade provides tangible economic, environmental, and social benefits for artisans and their families.[16] But much of this anthropological and ethnographic research focuses only on one community. As a result, it is very difficult to determine whether it is fair trade, increases in market prices for coffee, or some other variable that is *causing* these improved outcomes.[17]

But discussing the research on fair trade misses the point about the importance of these interactions with fair-trade farmers and artisans. After all, few, if any, of the promoters I met were aware of studies involving fair-trade communities. Instead, their support for fair trade was socially constructed through these trips. Through these extraordinary experiences traveling to developing countries, promoters met other like-minded individuals seeking to change the world through shopping. They felt part of a brand community that shared their own beliefs.[18] Furthermore, by seeing for themselves how fair trade impacts farmers and artisans, promoters were moved to buy into the efficacy of fair trade. They believed that their individual actions directly contributed to the well-being of the people they had met. They became more passionate about fair trade; their support was invigorated through these extraordinary experiences.[19] And, I have to admit, I was also surprised at how angry and frustrated I became after my emotionally draining experience in Nicaragua.

On my journey home from Nicaragua, I had a layover in Miami and spent a few hours at the airport waiting for my flight to Philadelphia. I felt different from the way I had felt after past experiences traveling internationally to Eastern Europe and Canada. This time, the advertisements in the airport felt more ostentatious; the clothing worn by people in Miami felt more garish. I felt incredibly judgmental of the people around me. As a woman walked her overweight dog in the airport, I noticed that the dog was wearing a fake diamond necklace. I felt incredibly angry at this woman. The dog's collar disgusted me. I could not quite pinpoint why I was so frustrated, but I thought, "Doesn't she know about what is going on in the rest of the world? Why would she waste her money on this collar when people are dying of malnutrition?"

I sat in an airport restaurant by myself and splurged on a few drinks and dinner. Although a big fan of beans and rice, I was excited to finally eat a meal that contained neither of these options. When my check arrived, the bill was $36 for two drinks, French fries, and a sandwich. I felt sick to my stomach when I realized that my meal cost more than a worker would earn for ten days' minimum-wage work in Nicaragua. For weeks after the trip, I continued to make these kinds of comparisons. To compound matters, I arrived home right before Christmas, when the excesses of American consumer culture are on full display.

As my research progressed, I continued to interview people through-out the fair-trade movement. Many of the promoters returning home from trips to developing countries told me stories about "refusing to go to the mall for two years" and "only giving gifts of charitable donations during the holidays." Others talked about their "boycotts" of stores they did not believe were ethical. But a larger percentage of the people with whom I met, those I refer to as conscientious consumers, had never interacted with a fair-trade farmer or artisan. They talked about the many contradictions between their values and their purchases. Consci-entious consumers would say things like, "I hate Walmart . . . but last week when I *had to go* to Walmart. . . ." As I explain in the next chapter, conscientious consumers confront more contradictions while shopping than do promoters. In chapter 4, I explain how they make sense of these moral hazards.

4

"Who Are We Pillaging from This Time?"

Managing Value Contradictions in Shopping

He who can buy bravery is brave, though a coward. As money is not exchanged for any one specific quality, for any one specific thing, or for any particular human essential power, but for the entire objective world of man and nature, from the standpoint of its possessor it therefore serves to exchange every property for every other, even contradictory, property and object: it is the fraternization of impossibilities. It makes contradictions embrace.

—Karl Marx, *Economic and Philosophic Manuscripts of 1844*

Members of the Ten Thousand Villages marketing department make all their crucial decisions by asking one simple question: "What would Gwen do?" Would Gwen purchase this red vase inscribed with hand-written Bengali script? Would she like these ebony-inlaid silver hook earrings? Or would she prefer a red leather purse designed to look like a cat? Gwen is a thirty-six-year-old mother with a child in preschool who works as an associate professor at a local university. She and her husband have a combined income of more than $90,000 a year. She likes to travel, read, and practice yoga. Gwen and her husband each work hectic schedules but find time to volunteer in the community and support environmental initiatives. But Gwen is not a real person. She is the "ideal-typical" Ten Thousand Villages customer, constructed from an assortment of interview and ethnographic data collected by market researchers at a Ten Thousand Villages store in Ann Arbor, Michigan.

Nathan, on the other hand, is a real person who likes to think of himself as a conscientious consumer. He is a thirty-eight-year-old English professor at a community college near Philadelphia whom I met at a Ten Thousand Villages store that sells fairly traded handicrafts from developing countries. Nathan prides himself on being a progressive person. He is a union supporter who drove out to Harrisburg with his six-year-old son to protest an antigay-marriage amendment outside Pennsylvania's House of Representatives. Nevertheless, Nathan admits to countless contradictions between his moral ideals and his everyday shopping patterns. Although he "hates" what Walmart stands for, he explained, "When you've got kids and you've got a household, it's very easy to just say, 'You know what? We're going to Walmart. I can't pay five times as much for organic toilet paper." Each time he shops at stores he does not view as ethical, he asks himself, "Who am I pillaging from this time?" Nathan likes to shop at Ten Thousand Villages, but he also buys handicrafts from stores that don't share the fair-trade philosophy. He knows that many of his purchases cause harm to the environment and, in his view, exploit workers. Yet he continues to shop for these types of goods.

Many marketers and journalists think that Gwen is the typical conscientious consumer. In many ways, they are right. The conscientious consumers I met are well traveled, highly educated, and wealthy. Women are more likely to identify as ethical shoppers than men. But my findings indicate that conscientious consumers do not rigidly align their moral values with their everyday purchases.[1] I found most conscientious consumers to be more like Nathan: somewhat critical of the belief that shopping can change the world but still willing to shop for a cause. Conscientious consumers are acutely aware of the widespread contradictions between their professed values and their everyday shopping patterns.

These contradictions are the focus of this chapter. In the sections that follow, I explain how consumers make sense of their moral identities while shopping, and I describe the strategies they deploy to manage these contradictions. I begin the chapter by focusing on the significance of contradictions in consumer behavior, and then I turn to the ways consumers make sense of these discrepancies.

Managing Contradictions

As advertisers continue to promote their fair-trade, sustainable, green, and socially responsible products, consumers gain greater opportunities to express their moral identities through shopping. They can buy hybrid and electric cars, light-emitting diode (LED) and compact fluorescent lights, fair-trade and shade-grown coffee, and Product (RED) and sweatshop-free clothing. Survey research shows that consumers are increasingly attracted to socially responsible alternatives, and many say they are willing to pay a premium for these types of products.[2] In the midst of this ethical turn in markets, interest in socially responsible products seems to be at an all-time high.

Given these trends, I expected conscientious consumers to proudly talk about the empowered Indian artisans weaving the popular "tree of life" wall hanging at Ten Thousand Villages. I thought they would discuss the merits of buying fair-trade coffee from farmers working in cooperatives or describe the enormous surpluses that Alex's Lemonade Stand has generated for cancer research. But this rarely happened. Instead, conscientious consumers deflected attention from ethical issues and toward the functionality of the wall hanging ("It matches the décor of the room") and the quality of fair-trade coffee ("It just tastes better").[3] Instead of talking about the benefits of cooperatives for Nicaraguan coffee farmers, they told me how the coffee was priced "competitively" with other high-quality coffees. In essence, they were hesitant to talk about any of the ethical issues surrounding shopping.

Over time, I came to realize that this was an impression-management strategy.[4] Conscientious consumers strive to appear to be altruistic (see chapter 5), but they do not want to seem "too preachy" when talking about how other people "should" shop.[5] Perhaps more important, appearing altruistic is just one of many concerns that affect consumers. They also want high-quality and functional products that are reasonably priced. If these products come with some form of green or fair-trade label, even better.

Survey research suggests that only a small percentage of consumers align their values with almost all their everyday purchases.[6] These shoppers, whom I refer to as promoters, treat fair trade and social responsibility as a "way of life." Each and every purchase serves to reinforce their sense of self. Rarely do these consumers shop outside their (relatively) rigid value system. Another type of consumer, whom I refer to as conscientious consumers, fits the profile discussed in this chapter. Depending on the survey, between 76 and 81 percent of American shoppers say they will pay higher prices for products produced under good working conditions.[7] But I studied a much narrower segment of this population that, at least occasionally, buys socially conscious products like Ten Thousand Villages handicrafts and fair-trade coffee. Whereas market research has described many of the characteristics of this type of consumer (e.g., Gwen), there is not much research on how these individuals make sense of the contradictions in their shopping patterns. There are a number of reasons these consumers are worth studying in more depth.

First, many consumer activists and well-intentioned critics argue that improving consumer education will lead people to purchase more socially responsible products. They say that if more people knew how fair trade benefits coffee farmers, they would actively seek out fair-trade coffee. Like Gwen, they argue, these consumers strive to align their moral ideals with their everyday purchases. But this view is too optimistic. Many of the conscientious consumers I interviewed know about these issues, profess to seek change through shopping, but make purchases that contradict their values on an everyday basis. Most consumers are more like Nathan: they like to feel good about shopping responsibly, but convenience, price, and aesthetics often compete with this goal.

Second, conscientious consumers make up a large and growing market niche.[8] This niche is especially attractive to business owners seeking to improve their bottom lines. Although companies may not care about social responsibility, they realize that they need to meet the demands of this large and growing population. As such, a growing number of advertisers have begun to tout the socially responsible aspects of all their products. Many companies simply began to promote aspects of their products that could be framed, even loosely, as "green" or "socially responsible." Maybe the most frightening example of this trend is the U.S. military's promotion of its "more environmentally friendly" bombs.[9]

The third and most important reason conscientious consumers are worth studying in more depth is that researchers still do not know enough about how they construct meaning, make sense of the contradictions, or become motivated to shop ethically. In fact, the critical study of consumption itself (as opposed to more instrumental, market-driven research) "barely existed a couple decades ago."[10] Among ethical-consumption scholars, some think this form of shopping could lead to a new type of global citizenship in which consumers think critically about how all their purchases impact the environment and the living conditions of producers in far-off lands.[11] In this model, consumption would act as a "rough democracy of buying" where citizens can "push" corporations to adopt more sustainable practices. Conversely, markets can also "pull" consumers into a more complex dialogue about social responsibility in the marketplace.[12] In this model, consumers can become vulnerable to "fairwashing" or "greenwashing" or profit-driven corporations. Scholars know that conscientious consumption does influence other social and ethical behaviors and may even limit other forms of altruism.[13] In this scenario, shopping becomes a modern-day form of tithing for guilt-ridden capitalists who then no longer feel the need to give money to other charities. Although this chapter does not provide conclusive answers to these questions, it does shed light on each of these issues.

Managing value contradictions while shopping is not easy. With countless options for each and every purchase, consumers need to weigh the relative merits of social responsibility against such issues as price, aesthetics, quality, and functionality. The remainder of this chapter seeks to make sense of the ways consumers construct, downplay, and justify their moral identities while shopping.

Earmarking Social Responsibility: Food and Gifts

The first way conscientious consumers reconcile the contradictions between their professed values and their everyday purchases is by earmarking. Earmarking is the process by which consumers assign particular meanings and uses to particular products. In *The Social Meaning of Money*, Viviana Zelizer describes how we earmark all of our everyday purchases, treating some as more valuable than others.[14] We spend money that we earn from work differently from money that we win from gambling. We are willing to pay more for an item when it is purchased with a credit card than if we pay for it in cash. In a similar vein but in different branch of research, social psychologists refer to one type of earmarking as "licensing."[15] Mazar and Zhong found that purchasing green products permits individuals to act less altruistically after the purchase.[16]

By purchasing a few ethical products, conscientious consumers relieve the guilt they feel when buying more exploitative goods, such as a T-shirt sewn in a Central American sweatshop. They set their ethical purchases apart from their more mundane purchases. Few exemplify this process better than Keri, a twenty-four-year-old professional cyclist I met through an owner of Mugshots Café, in Manayunk. The owner wanted to hire Keri as a part-time barista, but her cycling career required extensive travel. After meeting in a quiet corner of the café, I asked Keri if she ever thought about where the stuff she buys comes from:

> Yeah, it's pretty easy to ignore that, though. I don't always think about it. I'll look at a shirt and see it was made in Turkey or something. But I'd probably still buy it. So [thinking about where all my purchases come from is] probably a little bit down the road from where I'm at. The problem is once you get to the point where you're going to be this particular, that you will only buy organic cotton, hemp, or "made in the USA," or whatever you want to choose for your value system, it takes money. I hate to say that, but that's really the answer for a lot of different things. It's more expensive and . . . at this point I'm willing and able to pay more for good food that I feel is good. But I can't apply that for clothes or cameras or things like that.

Keri, like many others, strives to buy organic, healthy food whenever possible. Over time, I came to realize that food and gifts are the two most earmarked socially responsible products.

Jennifer is a hard-working and well-traveled owner of a fair-trade coffee shop. After a few informal meetings at various fair-trade events throughout the city, Jennifer agreed to sit down with me for a more formal interview at her café. This turned out to be a bit of a mistake, as countless customers and employees kept interrupting us to ask Jennifer questions. With my tape recorder turned on, Jennifer explained, in detail, the benefits of fair trade for Central American coffee farmers. She talked about the economic benefits for women, the low-interest loans for farmers, and the overall health benefits received by families selling fair-trade coffee. I was impressed by the depth and breadth of her knowledge.

When we finished the interview, I turned off my recorder, and Jennifer and I continued to talk for a few minutes. She mentioned that she thinks fair trade is important but that the wide range of organic foods in her café is more appealing to both her and her friends. When she tells people about her shop, she plays up the organic aspect and rarely even mentions that the coffee is fair-trade certified. "I just think people know more about and care more about organics." I learned that many other conscientious consumers feel the same way.

Karl is a conscientious consumer I encountered at Ten Thousand Villages. He earned his master's degree in community planning and was working in admissions at a large public university when we met. While picking up a few items at the Ten Thousand Villages store where I was volunteering, Karl became excited to learn about the products from El Salvador that we sold in the shop. He told me he had been to El Salvador and seen striking levels of poverty. He wanted to "help these people" by buying their products. After we chatted for a while, I told him that I was working on a project about fair trade. He eagerly agreed to an interview, and I met with him a few days later for a buffet lunch of Indian food.

Karl started thinking about fair trade, antisweatshop clothing, and other progressive issues in high school. He told me that it wasn't until college that he became an activist. He arrived at Miami University in the late 1990s, when the "antisweatshop movement was really big." Karl said he was "hanging out" with a few friends who "would talk about change but who wouldn't do anything about it. They were more focused on . . . partying, smoking, whatever and they . . . they would talk about these [progressive issues], but they wouldn't really ever do anything." Karl then "met a group of people who were completely focused on making the world better, who weren't partying at all . . . they didn't care about those things, and they knew who they were and what they wanted, and they were very focused on these issues." Karl said that changing the type of people he was hanging out with "made all the difference. You know, I'm hanging out with the pseudo-hippies that talked about things being different, and then I met other people who were sort of like hippies but not really, who really wanted to do something. . . . So I really shifted away from those people."

Karl is more knowledgeable about food politics than most of the conscientious consumers I met. He clearly elucidated the stress he feels in trying to align his ideals with his everyday purchases:

I still have issues with the organic labeling system itself, which is flawed. I'm glad it's there, but it's not, you know—why should I eat an organic tomato from Mexico? You know what I mean? Like, how much did it take to get me that—how much fuel did it take to get that tomato to me that's on my plate? You know, that sort of thing. Now, I still will buy them occasionally. I won't lie. I mean, I buy organic tomatoes from Mexico every now and then. But the cost—I'm trying to weigh is the cost worth it, and is it really organic once it comes to me from that far? What does that mean? . . . I mean, it could be certified [as organic], but not really be responsible. . . . There are loopholes in the organic standards and there are things that sort of water them down. You know, you can use things that are considered organic fertilizers that really aren't necessarily any better for the environment to be dumping them in large quantities and still having them go into the rivers and everything else even though they're considered organic.

Karl confronts what Barry Schwartz calls the "paradox of choice" every time he makes a decision about what type of food to eat.[17] We like to view the endless choices available to us as liberating, a way to find great value, and a way for us to express our true identities. But the endless number of choices leads to anxiety, stress, and even depression.

Karl's extensive knowledge of the food-supply chain is undoubtedly stressful. But he did not remove himself from the marketplace entirely, and he still strives to find food he views as socially conscious, as is clear in these remarks:

KARL: Yeah, there are some issues related to [organic labeling]. No system's perfect. I mean, I'm glad that it's in place, but unfortunately the price of organics—even though more people are consuming them than ever before—isn't coming down. Huge corporations like Philip Morris are buying organic farms up, so they're converting what were small organic farms serving a local area to these large industrial farms. Same thing with eggs. I started out—no, this is sort of my progression—I started out insisting on I would either buy organic coffee, or not even organic, at least fair-trade coffee. I wanted my milk to be organic, and my eggs. Those were the three things that I was most concerned with. Now people come to my refrigerator, and my cabinets are probably 90 to 95 percent organic. And, you know, part of me is not necessarily happy about that because unfortunately I don't really feel that I'm getting what I'm paying for. I really don't. I'm concerned that we're paying these high prices and it's really not being ecologically responsible or responsible for the farmers. Organic doesn't mean that anybody's being treated fairly on a farm, you know.

INTERVIEWER: So you're frustrated because you're paying for one thing but you may not be getting the labor aspect or the—

KARL: Yeah. I found that some people buy organic because they think it's healthier just for them and that's their only concern. Just because it's healthier for them; they don't care about everybody else. . . . [It's] not just because of my own personal benefit, although there is certainly that side of it.

Karl's earmarking of milk and eggs as food that needs to be organic grew into a more profound, albeit critical, relationship to organic foods.[18] And while I agree with Karl that many conscientious consumers buy organic foods primarily because of the perceived health benefits, I must acknowledge that there are other social factors that greatly motivate socially responsible consumption. Giving a socially responsible gift provides some more insight into these motives.

Gift giving is loaded with meaning. More than just the exchange of a product, it includes an exchange status, values, friendship, and supportiveness.[19] In gift giving, the giver negotiates a happy medium between what he or she feels comfortable giving and what the recipient will accept as a good gift. The conscientious consumers I interviewed, especially shoppers at Ten Thousand Villages, described in detail the meanings they exchange when giving a fair-trade gift.

Tim is a scruffy-looking, forty-four-year-old associate professor who commutes three hours to work a couple times each week. I met him while he was shopping at Ten Thousand Villages. During our interview over breakfast at a locally owned restaurant that did not sell fair-trade coffee, Tim explained what types of meaning are exchanged when he gives a fair-trade gift:

So yeah, I'm sure that with the gifts I bought at Ten Thousand Villages, I intentionally bought because I know my niece is trying to change how

she imagines her life. But she lives in a suburban strip-mall land, so . . .
I think she likes the store, and I try to support her trying to do that. So
that was a very intentional gift, and I know she'll read it that way and
she'll feel supported.

Tim explained that he thinks deeply about what he purchases for his
close relatives, but he later admitted, "When it gets down to the bottom of the list [of people to buy for] and cash is short, it's like, well,
you know, let's go to Ross [a department store] and see what they
have on their shelves in the back of the store—where they have stuff
to pick up for a buck." The thought process behind Tim's gift giving is
quite common among conscientious consumers. He wants to find that
"unique" and "meaningful" gift for those he cares deeply about but buys
products that are on sale or convenient to purchase for his more distant acquaintances.

Most givers of fair-trade gifts include a small card that describes
where the product was made, who made it, and how the artisans benefited from the purchase. The card makes the gift appear more significant and, one hopes, more meaningful. Marina, a forty-four-year-old
chemist with a PhD from an Ivy League university, explains:

> I always ask for the little card or the little brochure, and I'll throw that
> in there with the gift, so they'll know where it came from. And I always
> try to keep where it was made. I take the price off, but keep "Made in so-
> and-so" there, stuck on there. I hope they see it.

Nevertheless, conscientious consumers do not want to overempha-
size the moral implications of their gifts.[20] Emily, a thirty-year-old regular at an Independents coffee shop who works as a director of human
resources for a small firm, adds: "I think at Ten Thousand Villages,
sometimes [the gift] comes with an explanation. So I do like that, but
I don't throw it in their face. Usually you can tell that something came
from Ten Thousand Villages."

During our interview at the Greenline café in West Philadelphia,
Erin, a thirty-year-old sculptor, fiction writer, and instructor of aerial
acrobatics, went into more depth about not wanting to offend or inter-
ject ethical dimensions into the gift-giving exchange:

I prefer to buy [gifts] that are socially responsible. But I don't really feel like I want to force that on other people. So I'm going out and doing the buying and so I'd feel better about it if it were a fair-trade product or bought in my own neighborhood or if it went along with any of the practices I support, but I don't feel like I need to go tell everybody, "Look, this gift you're getting, it's okay. No one got hurt." You know? They can appreciate it or not.

Erin is not shy about professing her opinions and values to her close friends and family, but she feels that gift giving is not a proper occasion for proselytizing. This norm seems to be shared by most conscientious consumers but was most clearly articulated by Erin, who later told me:

I feel like gift giving is sometimes . . . it's more fraught than you would want it to be, with, like, "Oh, I'm giving you something and it has various meanings attached to it," or you want some response from the person. And then when it's you pushing your social agenda on them through a gift, then it just feels bad to me. At the same time, I can remember going and telling my family members sometimes, like, "Oh, you shouldn't shop at Walmart. You shouldn't buy Nike products." I will say these things, but I guess not in the context of [giving a gift].

Although conscientious consumers often do not explain the ethical implications of their gifts to recipients, they do take pride in their purchases. Karl, the organic tomato expert, bluntly explained: "I'm proud of the fact that I got it from Ten Thousand Villages. So it's a unique gift, it does have a conscience, and it's not just some stupid piece of crap that you get at Macy's or wherever."

They view their gifts as having benefits for both the producer and the recipient; in essence, it is considered a "double gift." Cynthia, a fifty-year-old college administrator who shops for fair-trade coffee and handicrafts, explained:

If I can make my choice between one place or another . . . I'm going to go to Ten Thousand Villages first. If it's a gift for someone, I'm going to [buy it] if it has a purpose, that it benefits somebody. It's like giving more than once.

Similarly, Francine, a forty-five-year-old regular at Ten Thousand Villages who coordinates community service programs at a local college, described an added bonus of buying gifts from the store: "Even if I choose the wrong gift, at least I'm giving something to somebody." Conscientious consumers take pride in the socially responsible aspects of the gifts they give, even while downplaying this part of the gift to its recipient.

"The Coffee Didn't Taste Good Anymore": Taste, Quality, and Aesthetics

In their influential book *On Justification: Economies of Worth*, the French social scientists Luc Boltanski and Laurent Thevenot seek a set of guidelines that explain the ways individuals justify their behavior in everyday interactions.[21] They show that individuals often appeal to higher "common principles" to forge solidarity, gain respect, and avoid friction with the people with whom they are interacting. Thus, when potentially polarizing conversations about issues such as religion, politics, or morality arise, individuals will redirect the discussions toward issues that they may both agree upon. During my interviews and observations in the fair-trade movement, I constantly saw individuals shifting discussions away from ethically charged issues in order to forge solidarity with others. Consumers tactfully steer the focus of conversations toward product quality, taste, and price.

Nick is a conscientious consumer who learned about fair trade in college while taking a sociology class on globalization. He graduated eight years ago and is currently working in the information technology department at a large hospital. After graduation, Nick landed a job in Center City Philadelphia and began buying his coffee at Cosi, a local chain store. But he was never satisfied with his coffee from Cosi. He knew the coffee was not fair trade, and he feared that the farmers were being exploited. Nick told me it was "really cool" to learn that Joe Coffee Bar sold fair-trade coffee. "So I didn't know it was fair trade before I came in, but after I did, it was like, 'All right. This is awesome.' And then, actually, incidentally, that's when I stopped going to Cosi. All of the sudden the Cosi coffee didn't taste any good anymore." When Nick learned that Joe Coffee Bar sold fair-trade coffee, he quickly developed an emotional attachment to its coffee. Although his motivation for continuing to go to Joe Coffee Bar was based on his allegiance to fair trade, Nick partly frames his switch in terms of taste. Many conscientious consumers justify their preference for, or even against, socially responsible products in terms of taste, quality, and aesthetics.

Fair trade is not, however, a reliable measure of how the coffee will taste. When fair-trade standards were first established, many of the coffee beans were not comparable to other specialty beans. Early entrepreneurs were more concerned with the fair-trade philosophy than with the quality of the coffee. Today, fair-trade coffee importers realize that they must compete with other specialty coffees. More important, coffee quality is based on factors such as altitude, rainfall amounts, type of coffee bean (arabica/robusta), and whether the coffee cherry was picked when ripe. There is no correlation between these factors and whether the beans receive fair-trade certification. Moreover, the supply of fair-trade-certified coffee is currently outpacing demand. As a result, a lot of high-quality specialty coffees are produced with fair-trade standards but sold without the Fair Trade USA logo. Whether or not coffee is certified as fair trade has no impact on how it actually tastes.[22]

Nevertheless, conscientious consumers often told me that their preference for a wide range of socially responsible products is based primarily on taste. My meeting with Marina, a Ten Thousand Villages shopper, illustrates this point better than most. Marina, who talked about giving a brochure with her fair trade gifts, is in her late thirties and was born in Bangladesh. I interviewed Marina in her spacious, one-hundred-plus-year-old home in Chestnut Hill. She identifies as a progressive person, has hosted Democratic political candidates in her home, and likes to buy organic and socially responsible food. During the interview, her dog began barking loudly, and this reminded Marina that even the dog's food is organic. Rather than mention the moral or health implications of buying organic, Marina noted the importance of taste: "[The dog] is the biggest consumer [of organics] in the house because she loves to eat organic dog food. She didn't like it in the beginning, but now, if she has a choice . . ." It's hard to imagine Marina's dog ever having the choice between organic and nonorganic dog food. But it's important for Marina to tell herself that her dog prefers the taste of organic. The focus on her dog's favorite type of food frames the conversation as an individual preference and avoids emphasizing whether others "ought to buy" organic food.

Keri, the twenty-four-year-old professional cyclist, is not afraid to strongly advocate against going to chain stores when she's among her friends. She feels guilty shopping at these stores and points to the quality of the food as further justification for her beliefs:

> I'm really that annoying person in the group when you're trying to go out to dinner. I'm not going to go to Outback or Friday's or Applebee's or any of them. I hate those places. So restaurant chains I don't like. The big guy, Walmart, I mean any of them. These are places I avoid at all costs. Not only because of the crappy products. I mean it's just, to me, a junkyard, which, to a lot of people, that's really silly.

Keri cares deeply about where she shops, but she told me that she fears looking too self-righteous when discussing the ethical implications of shopping.[23]

Even when conscientious consumers keep morality at the forefront of their reason for not frequenting certain stores, they still tend to mention product quality as a further explanation for their purchases. Aline is a recent college graduate and a fair-trade promoter who works for Ten Thousand Villages. She was working a second job at an Independents coffee shop when we met. Aline seemed skeptical about my motives for interviewing her, but she opened up and became animated when talking about places she does not like to shop:

> Also, all of those chain stores, especially the high-end but low-quality clothing stores like the Gap and places like that . . . you're paying so much for these things and yet they might fall apart two days after you buy them. And they are most likely using sweatshops and just overcharging the customers and then underpaying the workers.

Aline uses product quality to make a strong case against shopping at the stores she dislikes. Many consumers talk about consumption in a similar manner: they emphasize product quality and personal preferences instead of sweatshop labor, fair trade, or other morally charged issues.

Product quality is also used to justify shopping at places consumers do not view as ethical. Whereas Aline criticized the Gap because of the poor quality of its clothing, Adrian explained that she shops at the Gap because it sells high-quality clothing. I met Adrian while we were both hanging out at Infusion Coffee and Tea, another Independents café. I had seen her at the coffee shop on multiple occasions, and I asked her for a formal interview. Adrian's response came after I asked her if she ever thought about where the stuff she buys comes from:

> Yes, I do. And there are times, you know, for a couple of years I didn't buy Gap clothing. But then at the time their quality was such that five kids could wear the same shirt. And, actually, my five kids did wear that shirt. And so, yes, I do.

Adrian deflects attention from the moral implications of shopping at the Gap and focuses on the durability of the clothing. She is aware of the stigma that the Gap possesses in the eyes of many of her friends. And, since we conducted the interview while her friends knitted at a café table nearby, Adrian may have been hesitant to talk positively about a store that receives much negative attention from antisweatshop advocates. Further, our interview focused on socially responsible consumption, and she may have viewed me as someone who is critical of the Gap.

Stephanie is a thirty-something neighbor of mine who lives with her partner and their three-year-old daughter in Northwest Philadelphia. Stephanie and her partner probably would be married by now if Pennsylvania allowed women to marry each other. Stephanie is active politically and cares about where she shops. She refuses to go to Walmart, for instance, because of its poor labor policies. Recently, Stephanie learned that Target, a store that she "loves," had donated $150,000 to a strongly antigay gubernatorial candidate, Tom Emmer, in Minnesota. Stephanie explained that she "just can't give up shopping at Target. . . . I love the store." She admitted that continuing to shop there "would be hard," but she has no intention of boycotting one of her favorite stores.

Jocelyn is a promoter whom I briefly described in chapter 3. She worked for Ten Thousand Villages until she got tired of working in the retail industry. Jocelyn grew up in England, and, after finishing high school, she traveled the world in the British Royal Air Force. Although few people would guess that Jocelyn had ever been in the military, she explained that she was a bit of a "problem child" and that the military provided some much-needed structure in her life. Equally important, the Air Force allowed her to travel throughout the world. Jocelyn works hard to put her values into each and every purchase she makes. She has a long list of chain stores and brands that she boycotts—so many, in fact, that she has a hard time remembering why she boycotts each of these companies. She adamantly told me that she "hates shopping." She does, however, frequent a local cooperative for her groceries, Trader Joe's for meals that can be prepared quickly, and a thrift shop for her clothes. During our interview, I pushed Jocelyn about other places she shops. She eventually admitted that she likes to go to Old Navy. While blushing and seeming quite uncomfortable, she said that she really does "love the clothes and you can't beat the prices."

Lisa, who has a master's degree from an elite private university, is a conscientious consumer who loves to shop at Ten Thousand Villages. I met Lisa on a blustery January morning while I was working the cash register at Ten Thousand Villages. She agreed to a formal interview, and we met a few days later at Infusion. On the way to the interview, Lisa's daughter fell asleep in the car. So we talked in the front seat of her SUV with the car running, while her daughter slept soundly in the back seat. Although she spoke openly throughout our interview, at one point she seemed a bit reluctant to tell me she likes to shop at Banana Republic:

> I don't know if [the clothing she likes] is traded fairly, [or] what those people are getting for it. If I get them at a place like Ten Thousand Villages, I know that it's okay. But I also like Banana Republic. I think they have really fine-quality clothes. I can get great things on the sale rack. I guess that they probably have sweatshops, you know. I think they're affiliated with the Gap, and I know they [have sweatshops].

Lisa explained that she likes to buy socially responsible clothes, but she rationalizes her purchases of Banana Republic clothes by talking about the high quality she can get at a great price.

As our interview continued, Lisa discussed a few of her attempts to boycott stores she dislikes:

LISA: So I try to never shop at Walmart, just as a practice. Where else? So, like, another example would be—I don't know if you know down in South Philadelphia there's, like, the big cheesesteak kings, Pat's and Geno's. Geno's is the really flashy one that has all the stuff outside of it. And they put up this sign recently that says, "This is America. When ordering, speak English."

INTERVIEWER: Yeah, I did follow that.

LISA: Right. And then Pat's put up a sign that said, "We will serve anybody," basically. So I don't eat cheesesteaks to begin with, but if I were to get a soda or go there, I would never go to Geno's based on that sign. . . . So practices like that will inform kind of what I do also. I heard that Cracker Barrel was very discriminatory against gays and lesbians. But then we were on the road driving to Tennessee and sick of all the choices. I don't eat at McDonald's; I don't eat at fast-food [restaurants]. I think it's gross. So we were like, "Let's try the Cracker Barrel," and I felt really conflicted about it, because I really loved their food. If I'm on the road, that's the place to go. So I was sitting there thinking, "I could see how this could be really discriminatory." It has a very Southern Christian feel, you know.[24]

In addition to the irony of conducting an interview about social responsibility parked in an SUV with the engine running for more than an hour, this was a fascinating discussion. Lisa started this excerpt by saying that she *tries* to avoid shopping at Walmart. (I couldn't help wondering whether there was ever a time when someone forced her to go to Walmart?) She then expressed pride in boycotting Geno's even though she doesn't eat cheesesteaks. Lisa concluded with a discussion of the guilt she feels for eating at Cracker Barrel—a restaurant whose policies blatantly conflict with her professed values.

As I explained in chapter 3, after experiencing life on a Nicaraguan coffee farm, promoters often spoke about the high-quality coffee coming from that region of the world, saying, "It just tastes better." People like Lisa and most of the conscientious consumers, however, have not traveled to developing countries. They do not know farmers or artisans from far-off lands. And they do not know anyone who has worked in a sweatshop. As such, their allegiance to fair trade and to socially responsible consumption in general is a bit more tenuous. Conscientious consumers' motivation to seek out altruistic products is mediated by the desire, as one Ten Thousand Villages manager told me, for "pretty stuff." They want high-quality, aesthetically pleasing products. They want products that will make a great gift. And, not surprisingly, they are concerned about prices.

"I'm Way on a Budget": The Significance of Price

Aline, who previously mentioned her dislike of the Gap, tries to buy socially responsible products whenever possible but says that she is on a tight budget. In her role as a fair-trade employee, she emphasizes the moral implications of socially responsible consumption, but, when discussing her own consumption patterns, she points to economic constraints. Given her income and the relatively high costs associated with living in Philadelphia, it is no surprise that she explains her purchases in terms of price:

> So I try my hardest to go to thrift stores and places like Buffalo Exchange or used-clothing stores. Sometimes I can't help myself and I have to go to Marshalls or something to find stuff, because I definitely don't have a lot of money. Way on a budget. But I'd say my only really favorite stores to go to would be thrift stores.

Like many of the people with whom I spoke, Aline feels that shopping at a thrift store does not carry the same stigma as buying from a store that sells new clothes. Thrift stores are viewed as advantageous because of their low prices, but they are almost equally attractive because they allow consumers to reuse products that might otherwise have been thrown away.

Anna is a second-generation employee of Ten Thousand Villages whose father was a doctor. After graduating from college, she began her career at Ten Thousand Villages. During our interview, Anna explained that she considers prices when making purchases more often than she would like:

> I mean, I am very aware of trade and international trade. And so where I shop is very important to me, but at the same time the reality is I do

work for a nonprofit organization. And I'm not making a lot of money. So my resources are a little bit limited.

Both Anna and Aline cite their work in nonprofit organizations as justification for occasionally buying products that do not align with their values. Their relatively low income provides them with a "license" for not always buying socially responsible products.

Justifying purchases on the basis of price provides some protection from moral judgment. Chrissy, a twenty-seven-year-old graduate student who is a regular at Infusion Coffee and Tea, knows about fair-trade coffee, but she no longer wants to pay more money for specialty coffee:

> Sometimes [fair-trade coffee] is too expensive for me, and it's not in my budget. You know, I can't get the coffee that I like to buy, even though I was doing that for a while. Getting the coffee that's coming from the region where they're trying to help promote these people to have their own business or whatever, that they're not using bad practices. I was buying that kind of coffee in the co-op, but then I'm like I just really need to be cheaper with my budget and buy the huge can of Maxwell, and that's what I do now. I guess, in my mind, it's primarily financial. But that also shows you that I don't think it's that important to change my purchasing habits. I'd like to, but I don't.

In general, fair-trade coffee is priced competitively with other specialty coffees, but it is significantly more expensive than nonspecialty coffees. Chrissy's statement demonstrates one of the limitations of consumer education in influencing the purchasing patterns of consumers. She has become aware of the benefits of buying fair trade, but she has not changed her purchasing patterns accordingly. She mentions no difference in the quality between specialty and bulk coffee. As such, the price difference between the two becomes significant. Chrissy's allegiance to fair trade is not strong enough to disrupt her instrumentalist orientation toward coffee consumption.

Even many of the most socially aware consumers that I interviewed tend to justify many of their purchases in terms of price. Nick, who professed his love for the taste of Joe's fair trade coffee, now refuses to shop at both Cosi and Starbucks. He particularly "hates" Starbucks; he once led a one-man protest inside a Starbucks in Center City Philadelphia. Employees from the Starbucks were passing out free coffee cards downtown, and they began handing the cards to customers at Joe Coffee Bar, Nick's favorite coffee shop. A few days later, Nick entered the Starbucks and went on a three-minute rant about what is wrong with the corporate giant. Everyone stopped what they were doing when Nick began his loud speech. He told me that he became so flustered and angry that he "doesn't even remember" what he said. The Starbucks manager called the police, but, once Nick finished his passionate soliloquy, he simply left. Nick is deeply committed to living a fair-trade way of life; nevertheless, he explains:

> Well, sometimes you have no choice, you know? I don't like going to the Gap, and I don't go to the Gap. But sometimes I need a pair of khakis, and I don't want to spend sixty dollars at another store. And you know what? It still is going to be made somewhere else. So I'll go and get it on sale, whatever, get the pair of khakis. But I go to the Gap versus going to someplace else, then, based on political [reasons]. So, well, I'd rather go to the Gap than Walmart, because all of my money is going to be going to Republicans if I go to Walmart versus going to the Gap.

Monetary constraints, however, are not a great predictor of whether a person will shop responsibly. Adrian, the Gap consumer mentioned earlier, and her partner combine to make more than three times the national average for a household (more than $140,000 a year). She explains that she cannot always buy the socially conscious products that she likes because they're priced too high. "The fact is that if I could afford to buy natural yarn from Nepal all the time, I probably would. But I can't afford to do that, not with the amount of knitting I do. If I could afford to buy coffee [from Infusion Coffee and Tea] all the time, I would." A search for the price threshold where consumers could match their consumption practices with their value system would be pointless.[25]

Working Hard to Maintain a Moral Identity

With the growing number of socially conscious products available, from a cup of fair-trade coffee to an energy-efficient, LEED-certified home, it is logical to assume that consumers are beginning to talk more about the ethical implications of shopping. After all, survey research shows that consumers will pay extra for socially responsible goods, retail sales of green and socially responsible products are increasing, and survey research also shows that consumers are becoming increasingly concerned about the origins of the goods they buy, who made them, and how the producers benefit from the sales of the product.[26] But here's the funny thing: consumers are still reluctant to discuss the moral implications of their shopping patterns.

And it's not just mainstream consumers who go out of their way to avoid raising moral issues in their everyday conversations about shopping. Both the promoters and the conscientious consumers with whom I spoke, all of whom were recruited while shopping at fair-trade retail stores, worked hard to avoid talking about moral issues. They used savvy justification strategies to redirect conversations away from ethical issues and toward subjects like price, utility, quality, and taste. At times, they also willfully ignored talking about product attributes that would likely conflict with their value systems.[27] Many even admitted that they refuse to ask how clothing was made when it might have been produced in sweatshops. I discuss the ramifications of this lack of moral discourse in chapter 6.

Whereas many people like to think of themselves as altruistic and consistently try to position themselves as such, they also employ practices that negotiate, downplay, and even contradict this sense of self. Through selective knowledge of products and companies, the deployment of permeable understandings of moral issues, and the reframing of conversations toward an instrumentalist view of the market, consumers manage their roles as altruistic consumers.[28] Nevertheless, consumers do care about the social, economic, and environmental impacts of the products they buy. They want to influence their peers about these issues, but they do it by emphasizing product attributes, rather than by stressing moral imperatives.

5

How to Appear Altruistic

By 2007, the Independents Coffee Cooperative was up and running. It had a stylish logo, a strong fund-raising presence within the nonprofit community, and even an advertising campaign that promoted its fair trade and socially conscious cafés. The positive attention it was receiving as well as its emphasis on ethical shopping frustrated Todd Carmichael, a prominent local coffee-shop competitor, who was quoted in a local newspaper:

> Some are like, "Buy my coffee because I don't slap my wife." Dude, come on. . . . Of course you don't slap your wife. Of course I do fair trade. Of course I belong to an alliance. Of course I try to offset my carbon footprint. Because I'm a human being, you know? On a larger level, it's the way everyone should behave. It comes with the territory.[1]

At the time, Carmichael was not selling any fair-trade coffee, but he was running a very successful coffee business that was trying to help coffee farmers. In this quotation, he seemed threatened by his competitors' explicit emphasis on social responsibility. Intuitively, he seems to understand that altruism is socially constructed in relation to other acts of altruism. In other words, if the Independents Coffee Cooperative is starting to promote its fair-trade and socially responsible practices, his company has to defend its own behavior and assure customers that it is also acting in a moral manner.[2] Similar competitions for altruism play out all the time in the fair-trade market; the quest for altruism is a competitive sport.

During this ethical turn in markets, the cultivation of a moral reputation is especially important. Because altruism is defined within markets relationally, not everyone can win this competition.[3] The French sociologist Pierre Bourdieu calls the space in which this competition takes place a "field."[4] Within this field (or market), organizations are competing to maintain an economic and cultural (altruistic) niche. The field is dynamic, so, if one organization raises the bar for fair trade standards, others must adjust accordingly to maintain their position. Companies that are very profitable are rarely able to also appear altruistic.[5]

Examples abound. Many conscientious consumers believe that buying organic food is no longer as socially responsible or trendy as buying locally sourced products. Conscientious consumers told me that the U.S. Department of Agriculture's (USDA) organic standards are "watered down," and they do not like the fact that large, profit-driven corporations can sell organic products. As some of my interviewees mentioned, "local is the new organic." Within the fair-trade movement, a similar process is occurring with Fair Trade USA. The organization had been a pillar of the movement, endorsed by most fair traders as the primary certifier of fair trade products in the United States. But, as the market for fair trade products has grown and as Fair Trade USA has aligned itself with the profit-driven wing of the market, criticism of this organization has increased. As the organic and fair-trade markets have grown, the moral capital obtained by buying organic or products certified by Fair Trade USA has decreased.

In some ways, this competition for altruism can be viewed as a good thing. As Western consumers and corporations seek to enhance their status, far-off farmers and artisans should reap the economic rewards. Those who are winning the competition for altruistic status should be helping the most people in the best possible way. But, unfortunately, there is a big disjuncture between the competition for status within the fair-trade marketplace and the actual, material benefits received by fair trade producers.

The psychologist Steven Pinker makes a similar point when explaining whether Americans would view Mother Teresa, Bill Gates, or Norman Borlaug as the most admirable person:

> For most people, it's an easy question. Mother Teresa, famous for ministering to the poor in Calcutta, has been beatified by the Vatican, awarded the Nobel Peace Prize and ranked in an American poll as the most admired person of the 20th century. Bill Gates, infamous for giving us the Microsoft dancing paper clip and the blue screen of death, has been decapitated in effigy in "I Hate Gates" Web sites and hit with a pie in the face. As for Norman Borlaug . . . who the heck is Norman Borlaug?[6]

The answer is not as black and white as it initially appears to most. Norman Borlaug, considered the father of the "green revolution," used agricultural science "to reduce world hunger . . . [and he] has been credited with saving a billion lives, more than anyone else in history." Gates, in a stereotypical geeky fashion, crunched numbers to find out where his money could do the most good in the world. His foundation has helped alleviate suffering associated with malaria, diarrhea, and parasites throughout the developing world. Mother Teresa "extolled the virtue of suffering and ran her well-financed missions accordingly: their sick patrons were offered plenty of prayer but harsh conditions, few analgesics and dangerously primitive medical care." Pinker's point is that moral reputations often differ greatly from actual accomplishments. "Our heads can be turned by an aura of sanctity, distracting us from a more objective reckoning of the actions that make people suffer or flourish. It seems we may all be vulnerable to moral illusions."

During my research, I found that consumers play many games in order to maintain their personal identity and social status as conscientious consumers. Many know how to look socially conscious when giving a gift or interacting with friends and families. But few advocate or talk about social responsibility in more public spheres (see chapter 4).[7] Most shoppers are comforted by the thought that their purchases improve the world in some small measure, but they don't spend much time educating themselves about the "cultural biography" of the product itself.[8] They tend to possess only superficial knowledge about how their everyday purchases impact the environment and the workers who made the products. They also willfully ignore learning about products that conflict with their value systems.[9]

This chapter adopts a different tone from the rest of this book. The purposefully provocative style is not meant to offend. By making light of the status competition among ethical shoppers, I strive to redirect our focus toward the material implications of our everyday purchases. If consumers really care about the economic, environmental, and social conditions of producers, then they need to seriously reconsider their shopping patterns and make radical changes in how they shop. After outlining the three rules required to appear altruistic, I conclude with a brief discussion of some of the celebrities of the ethical-shopping community. I contrast their seemingly radical agendas with those of the typical conscientious consumer and discuss the extent to which shopping acts as a meaningful form of civic engagement.

How to *Appear* to Be a Conscientious Consumer

Consumers both create and are created by the ethical turn of markets. Consumer activists "push" companies to adopt more sustainable policies, and markets promoting sustainability "pull" more mainstream consumers into an environment that encourages them to consider the social, environmental, and economic impacts of all their purchases.[10] The roots of this turn in consumer culture run deep; there is a long history in the United States of social movements linking consumption and morality.[11] The Montgomery bus boycotts, protests against General Motors' safety policies, support for union-made products, and the antiapartheid divestment movement are just the tip of the iceberg. The mainstreaming of these markets is what is new. The number of boycotts increased substantially in the late 1990s, and the ways consumers could "shop for a cause" also increased dramatically.[12] Instead of a small group of social movement participants advocating for a cause, a growing number of mainstream consumers are seeking change through markets. Since there are an increasing number of ways for consumers to express their moral identities through shopping, I decided to present a few quick-and-dirty strategies to help shoppers meet this goal.

In the vein of popular "How to" books, I describe three steps shoppers must follow to win the competition for altruistic status. This competition is about appearance; it is not really about doing the most good. The strategies presented here are all based on techniques utilized by conscientious consumers and promoters who seek out fair-trade products. The first step is relatively easy to take: boycott a prominent market leader. During my interviews, Walmart received more negative attention than any other company. Most aspiring conscientious consumers are hardwired to boycott this store. They found it easy to stigmatize Walmart's price-sensitive marketing strategies, which have little interest in issues like ethics or social responsibility. The second step is a bit more difficult: lead a moral crusade against a fair-, sweat-, or greenwashing company. For the conscientious consumers I met, this meant criticizing Starbucks. Starbucks built its reputation, at least in part, by positioning itself as a good global citizen. Seeing through the false promises of a fairwashing company is essential to win status among conscientious consumers. The final step is, by far, the hardest one to take. It is a step that is more often reserved for promoters. It requires shoppers to tell exotic stories about the producers of the products they buy. To do this, shoppers must obtain firsthand knowledge about the economic, environmental, and social impacts of consumption. As I explain, even the most steadfast conscientious consumers are often reluctant to take this step.

Step 1: Boycott the Market Leader and Change the World

In short, big is bad. In the 1990s, the Gap, Nike, and McDonald's all dominated their respective markets. They were also the focus of harsh ethical criticism. The Gap and Nike were accused of relying on sweatshops that had no regard for workers' rights.[13] McDonald's was criticized for its unhealthy menus and for its unrelenting focus on efficiency, rationality, and profits.[14] The competitors of these market leaders, often producing similar products and espousing similar corporate philosophies, largely escaped these criticisms. In order to appear altruistic, consumers must begin by condemning the most profitable market leaders to like-minded, socially responsible shoppers. They should disregard the policies of the competition and direct all their criticism at the frontrunners.

When I began my research on socially responsible customers, store owners, and consumer activists, I quickly learned about the evils of Walmart. People showered me with well-intentioned but clichéd lines: Walmart destroys small towns; Walmart promotes sweatshops abroad; and Walmart treats U.S. workers poorly by denying them health care and paying low wages. Others told me that Walmart symbolizes everything that is wrong with capitalism. In almost all instances, these criticisms were centered on Walmart's lack of respect for communities.

Not surprisingly, Walmart has a way of defending itself from these critics. In 2006, Walmart commissioned a study that showed that American families could save $2,500 a year by shopping at its stores. The study was promoted and discussed and critiqued within the media. By 2007, executives believed the findings were powerful enough to switch the companies' slogan from "Always low prices" to "Save money. Live better."[15] Whereas critics were attacking Walmart's self-professed disregard for social issues, the company itself advocated the benefits for the individual and her family.

Melissa, whom I met at Infusion Coffee and Tea, told me her "Walmart story" only after we finished our interview and I turned off my tape recorder. (I introduced Melissa in chapter 1 as the shopper who spent $5 for a T-shirt at Walmart so that she could justify buying expensive organic oranges at Whole Foods Market.) Melissa grew up in a working-class family that regularly shopped at Walmart. She now lives in a bohemian neighborhood in Northwest Philadelphia, where Walmart is looked upon as a shameless company by many of her friends. Melissa spoke critically of her own shopping patterns, acknowledging the problems she encounters while trying to shop ethically. A few weeks before our interview, Melissa went to Walmart with her daughter before driving back to Infusion (the fair-trade café where we conducted our interview). Once inside the café, she realized that she still had her Walmart bag with her and became "very embarrassed." With her bag in hand, Melissa *felt* the disapproving glares of other people in the coffee shop. Melissa acknowledged feeling "guilty" shopping at Walmart with her daughter, and that guilt intensified when she entered her local fair-trade coffee shop.

Other consumers took great pride in avoiding Walmart. They told me they could "not even remember" the last time they "set foot" in a Walmart. In one memorable interview, a consumer I met at Ten Thousand Villages told me his Walmart story. Eric only recently became interested in fair-trade products after a member of his church gave him a gift from Ten Thousand Villages. I asked Eric, a pastor in his late twenties who only recently moved to the East Coast to work at a large church, if there are any places he does not shop at:

> and this isn't just a trendy thing—but we [referring to his wife and himself] don't shop at Walmart. Just having done a lot of study in terms of practices, treatment of employees, sweatshops, and things like that. So, if we're going to go to a big-box store, we'd go to Target instead. Now they're in the news recently there's a lot of more of like Target coming up in terms of —you know, Walmart certainly is like the worst, but there are some things at Target that are raising some eyebrows for us right now that we're like, "Wow." . . . But we haven't been to Walmart probably in three years. And that isn't something we brag about, tell many people about. As a pastor, I don't stand up and say, 'You shouldn't shop at Walmart.' I really hate when pastors do that.

Although he is in a leadership position within his church, he fears sounding too preachy to the members of his congregation.

For many conscientious consumers, boycotting Walmart is an extremely important marker of their identity. I met Sabrina, a sixty-three-year-old teacher of gifted students in a suburban elementary school, while she was shopping at Ten Thousand Villages. I asked her whether she drinks coffee:

> SABRINA: All the time.
> INTERVIEWER: But not fair trade in general?
> SABRINA: It's just too expensive. We drink so much coffee. It's just incredible . . . like if we got it, we would save it for a special occasion. But if you can get Folgers for two cans for $5, I mean, it's—

INTERVIEWER: I think Walmart is going to start selling a fair-trade coffee that's priced . . . really cheap.

SABRINA: Well, that's good. I don't know where a Walmart is near my home, but that would be good. Boy, they're influential . . . I mean, I don't ever shop there, but it's such a big issue in the news and—oh, my word.

INTERVIEWER: So you don't shop there intentionally? I mean, not just because they're not near your house?

SABRINA: No. Walmart has such bad press about how it treats its personnel. It's incredible—making them work through their breaks and not giving them overtime.

Prior to this part of the conversation, Sabrina told me that fair trade helps producers make "enough that they [can] provide for themselves and their family's basic needs." In addition, she has helped sell fair-trade coffee at her church. In other words, Sabrina knows about the importance of fair trade for impoverished coffee farmers. She has no problem buying coffee grown by farmers working on a plantation with poor working conditions, but she could not even fathom shopping at Walmart.

A number of fair-trade consumers explained that they learned about the evils of Walmart. Most notably, they mentioned articles in the *New York Times*, movies such as *Walmart: The High Cost of Low Price* (2005), and books such as Barbara Ehrenreich's *Nickel and Dimed* (2001) as being especially influential. Ironically enough, these same consumers explained that they know little or nothing about the working conditions at Target, a place they frequently shop. Adrian, a fifty-year-old social worker who regularly hangs out at Infusion, makes this point succinctly: "I really do try to make socially responsible decisions when I know and when I'm aware. If I'm not aware, [then] whatever." Just like most people I met during my research for this book, Adrian willfully avoids questioning her relationship to Target because the answers do not align with her self-image.

Chrissy's reaction to Walmart is also typical of the conscientious consumers that I met. Chrissy is in graduate school at a private university and regularly studies at Infusion Coffee and Tea. One day at Infusion, I saw her skimming the Fair Trade USA (at the time "Transfair") website for information about fair trade. The conversational opening was already in place, so I approached her to talk about ethical shopping. Chrissy is a conscientious consumer who no longer shops at Walmart because she dislikes the working conditions of its employees. But, like Adrian, she consciously avoids learning about the policies of one of her favorite stores, Target. It could be that Target's policies receive less critical attention in the mass media (very likely), or it could be that Chrissy simply does not want to learn more about a store she likes:

> Although this does seem slightly hypocritical, I wouldn't shop at Walmart. That's one store that I would not shop there, but that's only because I do know things about Walmart and their practices. I, on the other hand, do not take the time to look up all of the practices of the stores that I do go to. I think I have looked up Target, but not in enough detail.

Among conscientious consumers, Target is perceived as a more socially conscious alternative to Walmart. It seems that conscientious consumers are earmarking mass-produced items (e.g., beauty products, cleaning supplies) as acceptable purchases at big-box chain stores. Once justified, consumers view Walmart as simply price conscious and Target as a more responsible alternative. By avoiding Walmart, these consumers can feel good about their purchases. But, in terms of social responsibility, I wondered, is it acceptable to shop at Target?

According to CorpWatch.org, a corporate watchdog website, entry-level employees at Target and Walmart make approximately the same amount of money. A survey conducted in Minneapolis by the United Food and Commercial Workers union (UFCW) found that entry-level wages are "similar" and "possibly higher overall at Walmart." Further, "Target benefits packages are often harder to qualify for and less comprehensive." Critics go on to say that, "in terms of wages and benefits, working conditions, sweatshop-style foreign suppliers, and effects on local retail communities, big box Target stores are very much like Walmart, just in a prettier package."[16]

Elizabeth Ruppell Shell, author of *Cheap: The High Cost of Discount Culture*, makes a similar argument.[17] Retailers like IKEA, Target, and H&M want to distinguish themselves from Walmart. "Walmart can't escape its downscale connotations," so these other retailers carve out their niche by focusing on aesthetics (her argument) and morality (my argument). The emphasis on appearance reduces the stigma associated with buying low-priced goods. Shell, like members of CorpWatch, stresses that the emphasis on the bottom line is still remarkably similar:

> Walmart, Target, Lowe's, and the other Big Box discounters scour the globe for low-price suppliers from which to buy their low-priced goods. IKEA takes matters one step further: It designs to price, commissioning its suppliers to build not a mug, per se, but a custom-designed 50-cent mug; not a kitchen table and two chairs, but a custom-designed kitchen table and two chairs for less than one hundred euros.

Yet, the moral reputations of Target and Walmart differ greatly. Target has clearly won the battle for moral supremacy. There are many reasons why this is so. Walmart's advertising focuses almost solely on prices. It wants consumers to think primarily about how much money they can save by shopping at Walmart. The advertisements imply that this will lead to a better quality of life. Target's advertising takes a much different approach. Seeking a slightly more affluent demographic, Target emphasizes that renowned designers like Michael Graves create products specifically for Target. Its ads promote social responsibility by proclaiming that Target is good for communities. Near the entry of most Target stores you will see a sign that explains that the company donates 5 percent of its profits to local communities. And Target advertisers must love that their customers, partly in jest, pronounce their store's name in a mock French accent: "Tarjé." In short, they want their customers to buy into the notion that they are part of something larger by shopping at Target—that they are not the *type* of people who shop at Walmart.

The reasons I have suggested all seem like top-down approaches designed by marketers to convince Target customers that they are shopping responsibly. But consumers are not simply foolish victims in this story. They play an active part in maintaining the belief that they are different from Walmart customers. Conscientious consumers' construction of Target as a morally superior company is shaped, at least in part, by social class. As Friedrich Engels wrote, individuals, "consciously or unconsciously, derive their ethical ideas in the last resort from the practical relations on which their class position is based—from the economic relations in which they carry on production and exchange."[18] By "trying not" to shop at Walmart, middle- and upper-middle-class consumers can feel that they are morally superior to their working-class peers.

The essential point is that the moral reputations of these stores differ greatly from how they actually behave. At a minimum, I think we need to acknowledge that Walmart and Target are comparable. I acknowledge that there is a much wider array of variables that could be considered to objectively determine the extent to which each of these stores is socially responsible. I am also aware that Walmart has begun to offer more organic and healthy food options for its customers. Nevertheless, perceptions of altruism are relative, so, as long as Walmart continues its relentless focus on low prices, its competition can go about business as usual, largely free from the sharpest criticisms.

Step 2: Lead a Moral Crusade against a Fairwashing Company

Most of the conscientious consumers I met were highly educated and well traveled and had been raised in upper-middle-class families. They care about prices but also seek high-quality, aesthetically pleasing products with an interesting story. These are not the types of consumers who care only about low prices. On some level, they all care about social responsibility. To really gain status among this group, conscientious consumers must condemn a fair-, green-, or sweatwashing company. This step is particularly hard to take because, some critics proclaim, corporations do not have to conduct any socially responsible policies. In fact, the only goal of corporations should be to return a profit to their shareholders. According to this logic, even a small attempt at social responsibility should be free from criticism.

Starbucks has received the bulk of these conscientious consumers' ire. Starbucks helped grow the market for high-end specialty coffees by offering a quasi-public place to congregate away from home and work. Starbucks attracted the attention of bourgeois bohemian customers, or Bobos.[19] These consumers share countercultural ideals but also buy into the ethos of modern capitalism. Bobos are attracted to affordable means of class making. A (relatively) pricey cup of coffee becomes a

marker of class distinction, signifying that the drinker is more sophisti-
cated and discerning than the average coffee consumer.[20]

As Starbucks saturated markets throughout the United States and
abroad during the 1980s and 1990s, the company simultaneously positioned itself as socially responsible. It sold Ethos water to support
developmental initiatives around the globe; it teamed up with Product
(RED) to help fight AIDS in Africa; and it sold more fair-trade coffee
than any other company in the United States. But critics argue that
these initiatives were not sincere. Worse yet, they argue, such initiatives
simply served to fairwash movements for social change.

In *Everything but the Coffee,* Bryant Simon, a professor of history
at Temple University, pokes holes in Starbucks' ethical façade. Yes, the
Ethos water and fair trade are noble initiatives, but Starbucks charges a
price premium for each of these options. Starbucks donates five cents
to clean-water initiatives in Africa for each bottle of Ethos water that
it sells. But it charges twenty to thirty cents more for its bottled water
than its competitors. Despite the fact that Starbucks pays about the
same amount for its fair-trade and free-trade coffee beans, it charges an
extra $1 per pound for fair-trade coffee. Thus, again, it is the consumer
who is paying for fair trade, while Starbucks benefits both financially
and symbolically (from its enhanced brand image). Further, Starbucks
prominently displays its Fair Trade USA certification in its advertisements, but sells only a small percentage of beans with fair-trade certification. As I learned while conducting a focus group with Starbucks
customers, this leads some people to believe that all of Starbucks' coffee is certified as fair trade. As for Starbucks' environmental concerns,
most stores do not encourage customers to drink out of ceramic cups,
and few stores motivate their customers to bring their own to-go mugs.
Yet, on Earth Day in 2010, Starbucks unveiled an ambitious marketing
campaign in the *New York Times* promoting its in-store ceramic cups.
This advertisement made it seem as if ceramic cups were ubiquitous
throughout Starbucks, but Simon showed that many employees were
not even aware that customers could be given this option.

Among the conscientious consumers I met, those who professed the
strongest commitment to social responsibility said they "try to" avoid
Starbucks. They were familiar with Starbucks' attempts to fairwash the
fair-trade movement. Most expressed anticorporate sentiments and

therefore, as a matter of principle, could not trust a company as big as Starbucks. Many said they preferred to "buy local" and believed that fair-trade coffee-shop owners were sincerely trying to better the world. They liked that their local cafés displayed the work of local artists and filled their menus with locally sourced food.

By the mid-2000s, the Starbucks moment had passed. The retail giant was still expanding, but the coffee connoisseurs were starting to think of Starbucks as the McDonald's of the coffee industry.[21] The conscientious consumers I met were becoming skeptical of Starbucks' claims about sustainability. The most critical consumers questioned how much they could trust the CAFÉ practices initiative designed to provide a sustainable supply of coffee. (CAFÉ practices is Starbucks' in-house certification that its coffee is sustainable). For conscientious consumers, walking with a Starbucks cup was becoming a status liability, and criticizing the company was becoming fashionable.

Although I met many conscientious consumers who said they don't "like" or "trust" Starbucks, few shared an anti-Starbucks ethos as strong as that espoused by Joe, the owner of Philadelphia's first fair-trade coffee shop. Many people I met in Philadelphia's fair-trade community described Joe as an idealist, a strong fair-trade advocate, and a committed proponent of progressive social change. He supports many local charities. He promotes fair trade. And he advocates for organic and other anticorporate means of eating. His passion for food politics attracted the attention of a small but loyal group of customers.

Yet, Joe's hatred of Starbucks took up a great deal of his time and energy. At times, his anticorporate idealism bordered on the quixotic. Like Cervantes's famous character Don Quixote, Joe went on a quest to be viewed as altruistic that led him to throw practical means for maintaining a viable business by the wayside. Joe's quest for altruism, like Quixote's battle against the windmills, led him to confront colossal forces that he alone could not possibly defeat. In Joe's case, this meant locking horns with Starbucks.

In 2006, Joe's shop faced declining revenues and increasing competition.[22] To add insult to injury, Joe learned that Starbucks would be opening a new store less than a block away from his. At the time, three other Starbucks stores were located within a three-block radius of his store. Joe feared bankruptcy. With his back against the wall, Joe asked his customers to join him to protest another Starbucks' opening. Joe posted the following manifesto on his website:

> you may want to appear at the Washington Square West Civic Association governmental affairs committee meeting to hear a presentation by S . . . ucks, which is proposing to open another place at 1201 Walnut Street. Do you think having another one is necessary, just 2–3 blocks from all the others? Would you like having a McDonalds every 2–3 blocks from each other in your neighborhood? Do you think perhaps having this much density by one company is perhaps monopolistic and even predatory? Did you know in spite of all their advertising/marketing they only sell less than 1% certified fair trade/organic coffee—do you think dedicating 85–90% of all your promoting should be backed with a little more substance than 1%??? Then maybe you'd like to tell the community and the S . . . ucks agents your opinion.

At the time of this meeting, Starbucks sold approximately 5 percent to 8 percent of its beans with fair-trade certification.[23] Starbucks, however, was tightlipped with this information and would not reveal it to inquiring journalists. Yet, as Joe angrily notes, much of Starbucks' advertising centered on corporate social responsibility. A few advertisements even implied that all of Starbucks' coffee was fair-trade-certified.[24]

Before the big showdown at the Civic Association, I met Joe at his shop. I walked over with him and saw that a handful of Joe's regular customers were already at the meeting. And so were representatives of Starbucks. The company had sent a lawyer, a local store manager, and a small contingent of supportive employees to the meeting. In his speech to the board, Starbucks' lawyer explained how the new store would increase the local area's tax base and provide jobs for area residents. He also described the charitable campaigns Starbucks supported in the Philadelphia area. Perhaps foreseeing the debate to come, he cited statistics describing how Starbucks helped expand the market for specialty coffees. He explained that, in the 1980s, very few cities had cafés that primarily sold coffee.

The lawyer was right: the rise of Starbucks had cleared the way for other specialty coffee shops to open. But, as Naomi Klein, author of *No Logo*, explains, creating a market and cannibalizing a market are two different things.[25] Starbucks deserves credit for helping grow the market for specialty coffee. But, Klein explains, Starbucks tightly clusters the locations of its stores in desirable urban areas and college towns. New stores open and take away market share from other Starbucks stores. This strategy reduces the profits of individual stores but also discourages independently owned stores from opening in these areas. So, yes, Starbucks helped foster consumer demand for pricey arabica coffee beans, but the opening of a fourth store just sixty yards away from his café would in no way benefit Joe's business.

After the Starbucks lawyer presented his case, the Civic Association opened the floor for questions and comments from the audience about the proposed Starbucks. A medical student in her late twenties who regularly frequented Joe's store said she chose to live in Washington Square West because of the neighborhood's noticeable lack of chain stores. That the new Starbucks would be located right next to her apartment frustrated her greatly. Two other regulars at Joe's shop argued that Starbucks was "homogenizing culture" and would put independently owned coffee shops out of business.

Joe finally shot up from his seat. By this point, I had known Joe for nearly two years, and this was by far the angriest I had ever seen him. When he becomes passionate about an issue, he tends to go off on tangents; his thoughts sometimes jumble together. His voice cracked a couple times during his speech, but he continued chipping away at the coffee giant. "Starbucks is only concerned with profits," he said, then added, "They don't care about communities." As his face became flushed red, he said that Starbucks could "put me out of business." His thoughts blurred together, and he was unable to elucidate a clear explanation of why this Starbucks should not be allowed to open. Nevertheless, his ambiguous statistics about why Starbucks is bad for the neighborhood, coupled with his intense speech, captured the hearts of the attendees. The crowd of about forty people looked at him with respect while vigorously nodding their heads in agreement with him. Even those attending the meeting for other reasons seemed to side with Joe. Some even glared nastily at the contingent of Starbucks employees, all of whom sat stoically, eyes forward, looking at the members of the board.

A few other attendees expressed their disapproval of the proposed Starbucks, but, coming in the wake of Joe's impassioned speech, their criticisms seemed rather tame. Eventually, the board responded to the proposal. The committee chair made a point of agreeing with almost all of Joe's criticisms. She further chastised Starbucks for failing to meet the promises to the Civic Association that had been made by the Starbucks on Broad and Locust. (The store manager at that location had failed to install a bright light outside the alley adjoining the store.) For a moment, it looked as if the board might not approve the new Starbucks. Among the anti-Starbucks crowd, many people perked up; they started to think Joe might have been successful.

Ultimately, however, the board's skepticism was designed to appease the dissenting crowd and make Starbucks adhere to its unkept promises. The chair cited a recent article in *National Geographic Traveler* that proclaimed Philadelphia the "next great city." The author cited Philadelphia's lack of chain stores and its support for independently owned businesses as distinctive characteristics of the city. Newspapers and local politicians had been citing this article for weeks as proof that Philly would become the next Seattle or Portland, attracting a "creative class" of hip, young, and smart entrepreneurs who would shape the city for the next generation.[26]

Despite this public promotion of local businesses, the board members approved the new Starbucks. Before stating its approval, the board verbally admonished Starbucks. It made the Starbucks representatives promise to put a light at the Broad and Locust location. Then it closed by firmly saying that, for the foreseeable future, this would be the last Starbucks to open in Washington Square West. Joe and his supporters did not look surprised by the verdict. They seemed to suspect that their voices would not be heard.

Starbucks, Joe, and the board all sought the moral high ground during this debate. Starbucks positioned itself as an altruistic organization supportive of local charitable campaigns, one that helped open the market for independent coffee-shop owners like Joe. Joe countered by accusing Starbucks of having an overriding concern with profit. He mocked its claims of social responsibility. And the board, acting as the moral mediator, sympathized with Joe's criticisms. In doing so, the board curried favor with Joe's sympathetic audience.

As for their assurance that another Starbucks would not be allowed

In May 2009, Joe Coffee Bar closed and was replaced by a Dunkin' Donuts. Photo by Pamela Lowe.

to open within Washington Square West, the board members failed to keep their promise. Within a year, another Starbucks opened in the same district. Within two years, Joe had permanently closed the doors of his coffee shop.

Step 3: Tell Exotic Stories about Fair Trade

Fair-trade retailers strive to tell authentic stories about the coffee farmers and artisans who benefit from fair trade. These stories often frame farmers as empowered through consumers' purchase of fair-trade earrings or coffee.[27] But, as I explained in chapter 4, surprisingly few conscientious consumers repeat these stories to their friends and families. The authentic and exotic narratives may attract consumers to these products, but these same consumers are careful about how they talk about these themes during everyday conversations. Perhaps it is the complex and ever-evolving standards that serve to define fair trade. Or maybe it is a lack of clarity about how producers really benefit from coffee and handicraft sales. It may even be that some of the most beneficial aspects of fair trade for producers (access to credit, increased knowledge about consumer desires) do not convert easily into a sound bite or slogan. For those who seek to enhance their moral status, telling exotic stories about fair trade accomplishes this goal.

Ten Thousand Villages wants its customers to tell others about how artisans benefit from fair trade. Almost all the handicrafts come with a narrative describing the biography of the product. Consumers repeatedly told me that they take pride in placing these narratives alongside gifts for friends and family. The stories, which are printed on small cards, add value to the product. They emphasize how the product was made, who made it, and how purchasing the product will benefit the community where it was produced. Most narratives describe the artisan or group that produced the product and emphasize the gender or ethnicity of the producing group. This narrative of a children's puzzle is characteristic of many:

> Artisans at Gospel House turn local materials into colorful puzzles. Young men with little education or financial means learn new skills working with wood. Talented women carefully add the details using lead free paint, and in turn pass on their expertise to others.
>
> Albezia wood is a fast growing, renewable soft wood that is often used to provide windbreaks on tea plantations in Sri Lanka. It is ideal for wood carving.

This narrative emphasizes how men and women with "little education" use their talents and expertise to produce these puzzles. The fact that the wood is renewable provides extra value for consumers concerned about the environment.

This narrative goes on to describe how artisans who make these puzzles were affected by the tsunami in Southeast Asia during December 2004. Often the descriptions emphasize artisans who were particularly hard hit by prominent natural disasters such as hurricanes, tsunamis, or earthquakes. A goal of fair-trade retailers is to "put a face" on the people who make the products that consumers buy. Emphasizing a widely publicized natural disaster provides a strong connection between Western consumers and producers in far-off lands.[28]

By far, the most compelling fair-trade stories are told by those who have traveled to see farmers grow coffee and artisans create their handicrafts. After Joe, the owner of Philadelphia's first fair-trade coffee shop, traveled to Nicaragua in 2006, he came back to Philadelphia and wanted to tell others about his experience. A group of photographers who regularly display and sell their photos in Joe's shop asked him to give a slideshow presentation of his trip. Joe invited me to join him and to combine my pictures and stories of Nicaragua with his. We formally titled our presentation "From Co-Op to Cup: The Story of Fair Trade," but we jokingly referred to our presentation as Joe and Keith's "Dog and Pony Show."

About twenty people attended our presentation. I suspect a few felt compelled to come because of their business association with Joe. We showed slides of where farmers live and described the labor-intensive process of growing coffee beans. We showed pictures of typical Nicaraguan meals, of children playing, and of farmers working. We showed ripe red coffee cherries ready to be picked, and we included images of all the steps involved in processing the beans. Joe regaled the audience with a story about how he nearly slipped down the side of a steep mountain because of all the rain. Throughout the presentation, we interwove stories of how farmers benefit by selling fair-trade coffee.

Once we finished our presentation, a white man in his mid-fifties smiled deviously at us and raised his hand to ask a question. He said he was happy to learn more about fair-trade coffee but that he drinks only tea. Laughing, he asked us if there is any certification to help support "poor, virgin, thirteen-year-old girls who pick tea leaves in India." I'm not sure why he felt compelled to describe these imagined workers as "virgins," but his point was clear. Fair traders need to frame workers as impoverished, exotic, and needy to compel customers to support their cause.

There is a long history of coffee entrepreneurs who exoticize farmers in an effort to increase sales. In the late 1960s, advertisers at Madison Avenue's Doyle Dane Bernbach created the coffee icon Juan Valdez to "educate Americans about the origins of Colombian coffee." Early advertisements showed Valdez "with his mule crisscrossing fog shrouded mountains picking the 'richest coffee in the world.'" These advertisements were designed to create a distinct market niche for Colombian coffee by creating the image of an authentic coffee farmer. The goal was to enchant coffee consumers, making them think about exotic, far-off places where coffee is grown. The Juan Valdez advertisements were also designed to reframe Colombia from a "cocaine-infested battlefield" to a place where industrious farmers worked their fields to produce high-quality coffee. The ads were incredibly successful and led to a $1.6 billion premium for Colombian coffee farmers in the 1990s.[29] The Juan Valdez logo is still being used today to help Colombia's National Federation of Coffee Growers to expand the coffee market within Colombia, where locals drink half as much coffee as Americans. Juan Valdez cafés are also opening up across the United States to cut out the "middleman" in the coffee supply chain and to return more profits to Colombian farmers.[30]

I was curious about what fair-trade promoters thought about how farmers are framed in these advertisements. Personally, I felt very uneasy giving presentations about farmers I barely knew, living in places I knew even less about. Yet, I always believed it was important for audiences to obtain more knowledge about how and where their coffee is grown.

Although my goal was to educate, I can't deny the seductive factor of the images we presented. Showing farmers and artisans living in dire poverty made consumers feel good about buying fair trade. In part, it likely absolved them of the guilt they feel for participating in more exploitative forms of consumption. It allowed them to feel that they could make a difference in the world. They could exert control over a social problem. As Mark Moberg and Sarah Lyon write in their book, *Fair Trade and Social Justice*, "For consumers who embrace one or more of fair trade's transformative goals, its appeal, and no doubt one reason for its phenomenal growth, lies in its ability to engage a newfound sense of agency and identity through consumption."[31] Of course, this worked out well for fair-trade store owners who encourage their audiences to "buy more fair trade coffee."

Eventually, I got a chance to ask a representative from Equal Exchange about the group's advertisements. Because Equal Exchange is a worker-owned cooperative with a reputation for high moral values within the fair-trade community, I felt that its employees would be well versed in the discussion about the exoticization of coffee farmers. Sitting in a café at an organic grocery store in South Philadelphia, I asked Corey about Equal Exchange's use of farmers' stories in its advertisements:

> And I think it's interesting [referring to fair-trade advertisements] because I think it's something that's uneasy in coffee in general. I don't think that it's necessarily something that's uneasy for fair trade. From the very beginning, all the way back in the eighties [actually the 1960s], they had this 100 percent Colombian coffee brought to you by Juan Valdez. And there's this man with a mule and two sacks of coffee. And he looked kind of poor, right? It wasn't like he was in a suit, right? And that was just Colombian coffee doing some advertising for coffee that was in the grocery stores on the shelves next to Folgers. So that's something that's been pervasive since the beginning. . . . And it's a question of whether you treat that as a marketing tool or whether you treat that as a valid story of where your coffee comes from. So clearly Juan Valdez was a caricature of the person who comes through with your coffee. Is it more offensive to do that than it is to say, "This is don Francisco from El Roblar in Nicaragua, and he'd like you to know that your coffee helped his children go to school last year"?

Corey's comparison of Juan Valdez and don Francisco is very revealing. Juan Valdez has become a caricature of a real farmer. He is a fictional coffee farmer, no more real than a cartoon character. On the other hand, don Francisco is an actual person. Corey and some of his colleagues at Equal Exchange know don Francisco. Whether or not fair trade is an effective means for alleviating poverty becomes less important than the fact that don Francisco would "like you to know that your coffee helped his children go to school last year." Don Francisco's existence makes Equal Exchange's stories more authentic. His stories position Equal Exchange as more altruistic than its competitors who use images of farmers solely to increase profits. Telling stories about real people who grow fair-trade coffee is a higher status marker for conscientious consumers than telling stories about fictional characters.[32]

Some promoters take Corey's critique a bit further. Jesse is a nationally recognized leader of the fair-trade movement. He played a prominent role in creating the market for fair-trade coffee in the 1980s. Jesse is very bright and insightful, but he never hesitates to criticize the movement he helped create. During the Living a Fair Trade Life conference in Chicago, I met up with Jesse for an interview. Practically everyone at the conference knew him, so we had to find a fairly hidden location in the conference hotel so that our conversation would not be interrupted.

Jesse recognizes the importance of distinguishing fair-trade products from their free-market counterparts. These stories force consumers to think about how their purchases influence labor relations and the environment. Speaking like a well-read scholar of Karl Marx, Jesse implied that all consumers need to think about the implications for workers of *all* their purchases. He believes fair trade benefits farmers and artisans; at the same time, it forces consumers to think more critically about their everyday purchases. Nevertheless, Jesse is critical of how farmers have been presented in advertisements produced in an effort to sell more products.

Jesse believes that the framing of farmers as impoverished people simply serves to fetishize coffee, likely contributing to Americans' tendency to overconsume. "One of my biggest disappointments is that we have recreated colonial reality. We have refetishized commodities and iconized human beings and have turned fairness and justice into a brand. It all makes sense in the economic system we are in, and it is scary."

It is a Catch-22. Fair-trade retailers need to tell stories about artisans and farmers in order to educate consumers. But, in doing so, they dupe consumers into thinking that they have done their part to alleviate global poverty. Nicki Cole, a sociologist who writes about fair trade, argues that the consumption of disempowered, racialized, and gendered coffee producers is a modern form of symbolic colonialism.[33] Jesse seems to share this view, but he recognizes that this is necessary to get consumers to understand the importance of shopping ethically. Although often well intentioned, fair-trade advertisements and the fair-trade movement in general are not a salve for all that ails people at the bottom of the global economic hierarchy. As Jesse and other critics are aware, simply buying more socially responsible goods is not a sustainable means for saving the environment and moving people out of poverty.

"Appearing" without Actually "Becoming"

Americans love to shop. They treat shopping as a national pastime, and many ignore the growing number of social problems associated with this activity. Prior to the Great Recession of 2008, Americans had shopped themselves into debt. Net savings rates for households declined rapidly from 7.2 percent in 1990 to –.4 percent in 2005.[34] (Since the beginning of the Great Recession, there are signs this is changing.) By 2009, the average American household held more than $5,100 in credit card debt.[35] All this shopping is having devastating effects on the planet. As Juliet Schor explains:

> Ecosystems of all types are under threat. Humans are degrading the planet far faster than we are regenerating it. Deadzones are proliferating rapidly in the oceans; farmland is morphing into desert. Biodiversity is shrinking, and we're into the sixth mass extinction of species. If current trends continue, some scientists have warned that by 2050 the oceans will be devoid of fish, the primary source of animal protein for a billion people.[36]

Most conscientious consumers possess at least some awareness about the severity of these issues.

However, if you want to gain status among ethical shoppers, you must avoid talking too much about these issues. Discussions about how much waste Americans produce, unsustainable credit card debt, the social impacts of conflict diamonds, terrorist acts being funded by gold mining in the Democratic Republic of the Congo, child labor in the chocolate industry, the labor conditions of workers making the latest iPhone, or the percentage of money generated by pink-ribbon-wrapped products that goes to reduce environmental causes of cancer will get you nowhere.[37] Instead, talk proudly about boycotting Walmart; be critical of but not hostile to Starbucks; and carefully include a story about fair-trade artisans alongside the next gift you give from Ten Thousand Villages.

It won't hurt to talk longingly about moving to the mountains and "living off the grid." Make sure to emphasize your goal of reducing your carbon footprint, purchasing only necessities, and removing yourself from the work-and-spend rat race. Make sure not to tell anyone that these are simply unrealistic fantasies. There is no need to actually try to live this way.

Of course, these goals will only help you appear altruistic. If your intention is to actually align your values with all your purchases, you will have to work much harder. But your increased hard work may risk the status that you have worked so hard to cultivate. Instead of an ethical hero, you might be branded as crazy, an idealist, or even a communist.

There are a few minor celebrities in the ethical shopping world who are receiving both high praise and harsh condemnation. Annie Leonard's "The Story of Stuff" has been viewed more than 12 million times online; Colin Beavin's blog and film *No Impact Man* have received widespread attention (both chronicle Colin and his family's attempt to "have a good life without wasting so much"); and Bill Talen, aka Reverend Billy, has become famous in New York City and on college campuses for utilizing music, dance, comedy, and good old-fashioned preaching to stage "moral soap operas" and "retail interventions" in chain stores like Disney, the Gap, Nike, and Starbucks.

These celebrities of the movements for responsible consumption all do a great job of highlighting what needs to change if we are to live in a more sustainable world. Whether it is pointing to how much we waste every day or how advertising encourages participation in the work-spend cycle, if significant social change is to occur through the market, consumers must do much more than simply appear altruistic. But when I show films about Annie, Colin, and Bill to college students, I often hear a lot of snickering. In discussions with college students at the University of Pennsylvania and Saint Joseph's University, I find that many students emphasize that these people have "farfetched" and "unrealistic" strategies to alleviate social problems. The students really like their films, but the great majority said that knowledge about overconsumption will not change their current shopping patterns.

The success of Colin, Bill, and Annie and the growth of socially responsible markets make me wonder if conscientious consumers will begin to think more critically about how we are impacting the world through our everyday purchases. I wonder whether conscientious consumers, instead of being concerned about appearing altruistic, will seek more sustainable means of shopping. I question whether they really desire a more radical approach, such as greatly reducing their own consumption patterns. In the concluding chapter, I focus on this issue by discussing the limits and possibilities of socially responsible shopping.

6

The Great Recession and the Social Significance of Buying into Fair Trade

I am totally confident not that the world will get better, but
that we should not give up the game before all the cards have
been played. . . . To play, to act, is to create at least a possi-
bility of changing the world. . . . Revolutionary change does
not come as one cataclysmic moment . . . but as an endless
succession of surprises, moving zigzag toward a more decent
society. We don't have to engage in grand, heroic actions
to participate in the process of change. Small acts, when
multiplied by millions of people, can transform the world.
Even when we don't "win," there is fun and fulfillment in the
fact that we have been involved, with other good people, in
something worthwhile. We need hope.
—Howard Zinn, 2004

When I began this book, I sought to understand the pathways to participation in the fair-trade movement. I was also curious as to why
individuals want to support producers living halfway around the globe
when there are so many pressing social problems closer to home. I was
interested in the ways people discuss moral issues, and I wanted to
figure out how individuals make sense of the contradictions between
their ideals and their everyday purchases. Mainstream theories of
consumer culture and social movements provided the framework for
examining many of these issues. But I kept struggling to make sense
of a relatively undertheorized part of fair trade—the activities, beliefs,
and impression-management strategies of actors at the periphery of the
movement. Within consumer-dependent social movements, conscientious consumers occupy an especially important position. Their purchasing power largely determines the financial returns that are directed
toward specific causes. The limits and possibilities of conscientious

consumption, what I'm referring to as a "small act," are the subject of this chapter.

I define "small acts" as activities related to a social movement that are not necessarily meaningful for the participant. Small acts can include such activities as signing a petition, voting, calling a congressperson, or shopping for a socially responsible product. Both hard-core activists and those loosely affiliated with a social movement can participate in small acts. For some people, small acts are a way to reproduce their identity (as a feminist, a radical, or a fair trader). For others, small acts are a relatively inconsequential way of supporting a social cause. In other words, the extent to which a small act is meaningful is an empirical question.

Dana Fisher, although not explicitly working on the concept of small acts, provides an example of how meanings are socially constructed through political organizing.[1] In her book *Activism, Inc.*, Fisher shows how the increasingly efficient ways of gaining signatures for a petition drive (using cheap, outsourced, and alienated labor) serve to make the petition drive itself less meaningful. Thus, canvassing no longer becomes a way for individuals to create and recreate their identity as an activist; it becomes a small act, routinized and devoid of meaning. In the end, the progressive grassroots campaigns that hire canvassers gain a large amount of signatures but lose the committed support of these workers.

Fisher's research illustrates a subtext that is found throughout this book. It is not the act of shopping itself or the point of purchase that is necessarily meaningful; it is the social forces surrounding how we shop: how we give a gift, whether we can relate to the farmer or artisan who produced the product, whether we can imagine what it is like to live in a developing country, the extent to which we believe fair trade can make a difference, and our social networks. These forces all greatly impact the extent to which we "buy into" the idea that fair trade can solve social problems. For this reason, it is important for scholars of consumer behavior to go deeper and to understand the situational forces that affect the construction of meaning.

Fair trade and its closely related consumer-dependent social movements, including Product (RED), Alex's Lemonade, pink ribbons, and LiveStrong bracelets, rely heavily on the small acts committed by a large number of people. Although these movements all depend on a relatively small group of activists, store owners, and consumer advocates to set the direction of the movement, the ability of these markets to raise funds for charitable causes is contingent on the purchasing power of a much wider range of individuals. Thus, it is important to understand the impact of small acts by consumers who are often only minimally committed to changing the world through shopping.

Before addressing this issue, I explain how Philadelphia's fair-trade market survived through the Great Recession. I finished gathering data for this book right before the financial and housing markets collapsed at the end of 2008. The next section provides a brief overview of how the Independents Coffee Cooperative and Ten Thousand Villages coped with the changes resulting from the Great Recession. These changes yielded some important insights into the limitations and possibilities of small acts as a mechanism for social change.

Philadelphia's Fair Traders after the Great Recession

In the fall of 2005, I was hanging out in Joe Coffee Bar on a sunny afternoon. The store was largely empty, with only two other customers, both typing away at their keyboards. Joe saw me sitting alone in the corner and came over to talk about closing his store in the near future. He compared the end of his store to the death of Rasputin. Grigory Rasputin (1869–1916) was a Siberian peasant who became a trusted adviser to Tsar Nicholas II of Russia and his wife, Alexandra Fedorovna. Joe explained,

> First he was poisoned, but it didn't take. At dinner, he was poisoned again, but he continued to carry on in a similar manner—dancing and acting normal. He was then shot twice and knocked to the ground. After falling unconscious, he got up and was stabbed at least twice. He refused to die. He was then dragged to a pond, where he was held underwater until he drowned. But some people say he still lives today.

As if trying to convince me that he wasn't crazy, Joe smiled as he finished his story, saying, "Okay, I really do think he is dead."

Positioning himself as constantly under attack allowed Joe to play the role of the ethical hero. It helped him cultivate his reputation as a moral entrepreneur and helped relieve his frustration at Starbucks' predatory policies. Joe made this comparison three and a half years before his store closed. As discussed in chapter 2, many of the wounds to Joe's store were from external forces (its location outside a large residential community, increased competition, the closing of the Forrest Theater, the post–September 11 economy, and the Great Recession), but some were self-inflicted (the store's poor aesthetics and Joe's lack of business acumen).

After closing his café, Joe sold his eco-friendly row-home in Center City for less than the amount remaining on his mortgage and moved into a one-bedroom apartment. But, thanks to two customers from the café, Joe is still working in the coffee market. Those customers opened a coffee roasting company (Philly Fair Trade Roasters), which Joe largely runs. He is now roasting coffee for a growing number of cafés, restaurants, cooperative grocery stores, and individuals throughout the city. Although he believes he should have started years earlier, because "everybody is roasting coffee these days," the business is growing steadily. Joe estimates that his volume of coffee sales doubled during 2010. Sales will have to double in size again before he can improve on his income. Approaching the age at which many of his highly educated customers will retire, Joe is simply hoping to improve upon the $21,000 that he expected to make in 2011 and is saving money to pay a lawyer to officially file bankruptcy for his former business. He is optimistic that he will be eligible for some health care coverage through the Affordable Care Act proposed by President Obama and passed by Congress. Retirement, a former goal of Joe's, now seems like an impossible dream.

The other three founding cafés within the Independents Coffee Cooperative remain open, but there have been some significant changes. The original Mugshots Coffeehouse and Café expanded by renting space in an adjoining building. In 2012, the original store relocated a few blocks away to 1925 Fairmount Ave. The store is in an excellent location, with little competition from local or chain coffee shops. The café remains crowded, attracting customers from the residential neighborhood and from events at a nearby tourist attraction, the former Eastern State Penitentiary, which is now open for tours. The café also attracts foodies drawn to its local, organic, and cruelty-free menu. The own-ers of Mugshots also bought a café in Manayunk (a neighborhood on the outskirts of the city), which they have managed to make profit-able. In the fall of 2011, however, one of the owners felt the store was not growing sufficiently and decided to close that location. Mugshots also received a large development grant from the city of Philadelphia, which allowed it to open yet another café in a slowly gentrifying neigh-borhood in North Philadelphia at 28th and Girard. The owners also opened a store on Temple University's campus, at 1520 Cecil B. Moore Avenue. Although all three stores remain profitable, the two owners of Mugshots recently decided to dissolve their partnership.

The Greenline café now consists of three coffee shops located through-out West Philadelphia. The shop owners own the building in which the original café is located—a business decision that shields them from the rent increases faced by many other owners. All three cafés are lo-cated in a neighborhood that is becoming increasingly gentrified. The nearby University of Pennsylvania invested heavily in the neighbor-hood, encouraging faculty and staff to buy homes. The university even subsidized a local public school, which has greatly stimulated economic growth and property values in the neighborhood. Nevertheless, in re-cent years, the owners of the Greenline have seen sales stagnate. They have faced increased competition from other independently owned cof-fee houses, and one owner told me he thinks overall consumer spending is down. But there are no signs that any of the Greenline cafés are about to close. The Greenline continues to host local artists and musicians, and the cafés are a staple within their West Philadelphia neighborhood.

Infusion also remains open, attracting a diverse clientele of coffee lovers, parents, academics, and working professionals to its Mount Airy neighborhood. The owners of Infusion attempted to expand their business before the recession. They opened a small café near the Ital-ian market in South Philadelphia, but the business closed within twelve months. They lost a good deal of money on the venture: the location did not draw enough foot traffic, the costs of the initial renovation were significant, and the café was a bit too small to attract students or businesspeople looking for a reliable place to find a seat to work. Soon after the store in South Philadelphia closed, the owners decided to sell

Infusion to another young couple who share many of their values. The café remains open and retains a strong socially conscious ethos.

The Independents Coffee Cooperative formally ceased operations in November 2010. The cooperative succeeded in a number of respects. First, members were able to reduce their costs for a number of supplies by buying in bulk. Second, members educated one another on a wide range of issues related to fair trade and sustainability and, more important, shared general knowledge about how to operate a successful café. Third, the cooperative raised awareness about fair trade throughout Philadelphia. It hosted farmers from Peru and gave many presentations about the merits of fair trade throughout the city. Fourth, cooperative members funded an expensive solar-drying initiative for Peruvian coffee farmers. With the help of Equal Exchange, the cooperative created a blend of coffee called "Independents Peruvian Select." Some of the proceeds from the sale of Peruvian Select, as well as from a number of other fund-raising projects, helped pay the $12,000 bill for the solar dryers.

The cooperative eventually closed for a number of reasons. First, all nonhierarchical organizations involve intense negotiations. Decision making is often very time-consuming and can be very stressful for members whose identities are tied to the organization.[2] It was difficult for the time-deprived store owners to devote resources toward making decisions that required buy-in from the entire cooperative. Second, the economic tensions associated with a buyer's cooperative caused friction among members. A few members struggled to pay their annual dues. Others paid their dues but rarely attended meetings. And, finally, the cooperative grew very quickly, which put strains on the organization. Not all members initially shared the same vision for the cooperative. Some viewed it as a way to share ideas about how to run a café, others viewed it as a mission-driven organization designed to promote fair trade, and still others viewed it simply as a way to drive down costs by negotiating lower prices with suppliers. At one point, Independents accepted a member who was a strict economic libertarian, skeptical of all bureaucratic organizations. Although the member shared a fair-trade philosophy, he wanted to join the cooperative only to drive down his costs. Needless to say, this created conflict within the group. Over time, group members agreed that informal conversations were more beneficial than the cooperative itself.

Ten Thousand Villages is distinct from the coffee shops in that it is a nonprofit staffed largely by volunteers. The manager and the assistant manager at the store where I volunteered both left in recent years. In 2008, the store expanded its floor space by about 40 percent, taking over some of the space formerly occupied by the locally owned toy store next door. The new manager informed me that business remains strong, and the company has continued to receive positive press. *Forbes* magazine and the Ethisphere Institute voted Ten Thousand Villages one of the "world's most ethical companies" in 2008. In fiscal year 2010, national sales reached $23.4 million in the United States, a 2.3 percent decrease from the previous year.[3] Given the poor condition of the retail sector of the American economy in 2010, this slight decline shows that the company still rests on a strong economic foundation. The growing number of public events promoting fair trade (fair-trade towns, fair-trade universities, fair-trade month) will likely continue to drive retail sales at Ten Thousand Villages.

During the course of this research, I came to learn that the fair-trade coffee and the handicraft markets are distinct. Yes, both markets consist of consumers looking to change the world through shopping. And there was much overlap between these groups of consumers, many of whom shopped at both fair-trade cafés and Ten Thousand Villages. But, as a whole, more handicraft consumers than coffee consumers were committed to the fair-trade philosophy. Many coffee consumers were more interested in frequenting an independently owned coffee house that made them feel distinct from Starbucks' consumers. This difference between the coffee and the handicraft markets undoubtedly influenced the extent to which individual stores were able to remain profitable during the Great Recession. As I discuss later, the stronger emphasis on storytelling seemed to protect Ten Thousand Villages from some of the economic fallout associated with the recession.

The Social Significance of Fair Trade

This book has focused on the consumer side of the fair-trade movement. A growing number of researchers are examining the limits and possibilities of fair trade for small-scale producers.[4] Although tough to summarize, a few trends in this literature are worth discussing. First, the benefits that artisans and farmers receive from fair trade often do not align with the claims made by many fair-trade promoters.[5] Fair trade does not and probably will not be sufficient to lift producers out of poverty. The entrenched social problems in impoverished (largely agrarian) societies cannot be eliminated through the small economic premiums associated with fair trade. The reliance of developing countries on a single export puts them at the mercy of prices set in international markets.[6] Not surprisingly, countries that have relied on coffee exports are making efforts to diversify. With mixed results, some fair-trade farming communities are setting up programs for women to export handicrafts.[7] Farmers are trying to diversify their crops and invest their fair-trade premium in their children's education or other nonfarming-related investments.[8] At the national level, instead of diversifying, Colombia is trying to grow the coffee market abroad and within the country. Colombia has grown the market for specialty coffee and believes much more growth is possible.[9] The market for specialty coffees within much of Central America is small, so increasing demand may help stabilize the price swings many coffee farmers face. Further, the elimination of middlemen (sometimes called coyotes in the coffee market) has been replaced by the creation of a new layer of middlemen in the form of alternative trade organizations. Although the goals of these independent labeling organizations are noble, they still serve to filter profits away from farmers and artisans.[10] Nevertheless, researchers are largely in agreement that fair trade provides some tangible benefits to producers.[11] Most seem to agree that fair trade is a better form of trade than free-market policies.

As I finish writing this book, the extent to which fair trade can and should help farmers is becoming a hotly contested issue. The roots of this conflict run deep. In the spring of 2006, I was hired by the Fair Trade Research Network to interview leaders of the movement and to work with Jacqueline DeCarlo (Catholic Relief Services), Shayna Harris (OxFam), and Erin Gorman (Green America) to develop a roadmap based on interviewees' thoughts about fair trade.[12] We quickly found evidence of what many in the movement were already feeling—that there is a sharp conflict between those primarily concerned with improving the lives of farmers and those mainly concerned with growing the fair-trade market, which will lead to more premiums for farmers. Fair Trade USA wanted to grow the movement, whereas many others wanted to focus on providing more benefits for the farmers they were already working with.

A few years later, in the fall of 2009, I got to ask Paul Rice, the president and CEO of Fair Trade USA, about this issue at a fair-trade conference in Philadelphia, Pennsylvania. Paul had begun his presentation by telling his coffee story. His introduction to fair trade was remarkably similar to that of many of the promoters I met. As an undergraduate, he was interested in hunger issues, poverty, and international development. So, after college he bought a "one-way ticket to Nicaragua." He spent eleven years living in the country. His first experiences with development projects convinced him that he was only helping to create "increased dependency on foreign aid." He eventually learned about Equal Exchange and a few other importers from Europe that were calling themselves fair traders. After much prodding, he eventually convinced twenty-four families to organize themselves, take the leap, and join this fair-trade movement. After paying the costs of shipping and milling the coffee, these first families received $1 per pound of coffee, whereas the conventional profit they would have received for their coffee was about ten cents per pound. Word about the premiums spread quickly, and, with the help of many other mission-driven entrepreneurs, the market grew rapidly.

After he told his story, the session was opened for questions, and I asked Paul whether he was concerned that Starbucks and other companies were fairwashing the fair-trade movement. I also asked him, "What other tensions are you facing as you expand?" Paul explained the tensions he faced in trying to avoid watering down the value of the Fair Trade USA logo (at the time, TransFair). He then went on to discuss his relationship with Starbucks:

> The challenge for us now is how can we dovetail [Starbucks'] internal in-house program with Fair Trade? The fact that they've doubled volume in the last year is a really good indication that they're on a convergent path, and we could see much, much more of their product certified by us in the future.

He continued by explaining that coffee is not certified as fair trade when it is grown on plantations, but tea and bananas can be fair trade when grown this way:

> The movement in the past has chosen not to certify that sector. The industry clearly wants that. The industry would like for us to look at the supply chain and scrutinize whether everyone on that existing supply chain could be certified, rather than having TransFair say, "Yes, buy from that group." From a business perspective and, frankly, from a moral perspective, as well, it behooves us to evolve as a fair-trade model to a point where we can certify any farm, anywhere in the world. The current reality is that we can't do that. In the case of coffee, we're still focused on small family farmers. But, for fair trade to be more relevant for more companies, it has to evolve over time into something that's willing to give companies whole business coverage—meaning taking whatever supply chain they have and helping them green it or making it more socially responsible.

At the time, I had no idea how prescient Paul's comments really were. Two years after this discussion, Fair Trade USA ended its relationship with FLO, largely because it wanted to reduce inconsistencies in fair-trade standards and allow coffee farmers on plantations to receive fair-trade premiums. The subtext of Paul's response could be interpreted as an indication that he was listening intently to the needs of corporations, instead of farmers. And many in the movement have made that criticism. But another subtext is his sincere belief that this is the best way to improve the living conditions of all fair-trade farmers. He prioritizes greater consumer awareness about fair trade, presumably with the expectation that these consumers will be impacted by fair trade and become more concerned with supporting this cause. As I will explain, the extent to which this is happening is still up for debate.

These issues, however, are not the focus of this book. Instead of looking at producers, this book has examined the ways consumers construct meanings within markets for ethical products. Although conscientious consumers are often disconnected from these big-picture debates about the merits of fair trade, these debates do trickle down and influence conscientious consumers. In the following discussion, I explain the strengths and weaknesses of relying on shopping to generate social change.

Limits of Shopping for Change

Shopping is not necessarily meaningful. The founders of the fair-trade movement were storytellers. Edna Ruth Byler, the founder of Ten Thousand Villages, wanted members of her congregation to know about the living conditions of artisans in Puerto Rico, Haiti, and Pakistan. Jonathan Rosenthal, Rink Dickinson, and Michael Rozyne, the founders of Equal Exchange, wanted to teach their costumers about how American foreign policies were contributing to the plight of Nicaraguan coffee farmers. And many other mission-driven fair-trade promoters have gone to great lengths to attach meaningful stories to fair-trade products.[13]

But, as many fair-trade commodities have entered mainstream markets, the emphasis on these stories has been replaced by discussions of product quality, price, aesthetics, or taste.[14] For instance, McDonald's, Walmart, and Dunkin' Donuts all carry fair-trade coffee but rarely emphasize the stories behind that coffee. They seem fearful of customers like the one mentioned in the introduction to chapter 2 who just wanted "one normal coffee." They are fearful that highlighting fair trade could come off as a snobby display of class status. As a result, for many consumers, there is little meaningful difference between fair-trade and other specialty coffees.

The challenge for those concerned with growing the fair-trade movement and enhancing opportunities for impoverished farmers and artisans is to continue telling stories. These stories must include authentic narratives with a strong emotional appeal to consumers. They must avoid exoticizing or "other-ing" producers, while at the same time stressing the urgency of initiatives that are important for these producers:[15] clean drinking water, access to health care, improved education, and increased economic opportunities, at a bare minimum. Doing this without coming off as "too preachy" presents a significant challenge to those concerned with growing the fair-trade market. It is not, however, clear whether the meanings behind these stories can even be controlled. Molly Doane explains that, as fair trade moves from a niche to more mainstream markets, it becomes "refetishized."[16] The work that went into building and maintaining fair trade's social-justice initiatives is obscured, commodified, and neatly sold to consumers seeking a simple, convenient, and prepackaged way to create change.

It really is quite a curious situation. The current state of American politics is incredibly divisive. It seems that congressional leaders could not even agree on which way is north, let alone come to any significant resolutions on reducing unemployment, improving access to health care, balancing the budget, or strengthening the social safety net. The mass media are filled with partisan talking heads promoting overtly political agendas. Yet, everyday interactions among Americans tell a different story from what is in the news. Since at least the mid-1990s, Americans have seemed reluctant to talk about political issues.[17] They also seek to avoid raising political or ethical issues while giving gifts where the proceeds go to a charitable cause.[18] Even college students are keeping their identities in a "lockbox" to avoid potentially polarizing discussions during their everyday interactions.[19] The cause of this hesitation to engage in conflictual dialogue is unclear. It could be that negative political advertisements discourage participation in political discourse.[20] Or it could be that the sociologist Andrew Perrin is correct to argue that, "when people experience many conversations that have no explicitly political content, they learn that politics is a taboo subject."[21]

We know that Americans like to think of themselves as both similar to and different from their peers on the basis of economic, cultural, and moral criteria.[22] But why these attitudes are not explicitly put into practice in everyday moral discourse is a bit less clear. This conundrum presents an interesting research agenda for scholars of consumer culture who seek both an in-depth examination of consumer behavior and a deep engagement with social theory.[23] To what extent can consumer-dependent social movements pull consumers into a more critical engagement with the notion of citizenship? If the citizen-consumer tension is largely dominated by a market ethos, is it possible to make conscientious consumption more meaningful? Or will large, market-based movements for social change be confined to a sanitized version of social change that discourages consumers from looking behind the label to understand the political, social, and economic implications of shopping?

Fair trade carries a stigma that is unhealthy for the growth of the movement. For many individuals both inside and outside the movement, fair trade is viewed as both anticapitalist and antiestablishment. Some promoters railed against capitalism in their interviews with me, and many people I met who did not know much about fair trade characterized the movement as a leftist and progressive movement. The truth is that fair traders are working within the capitalist system of trade.[24] The movement is reformist; it is not promoting a radical overthrow of capitalism.[25] Mark Moberg and Sarah explicitly make this point:

> The contemporary fair trade movement rests on a deep (and perhaps deepening) paradox. Many consumers of fair trade goods are motivated by a strenuous opposition to the effects of neoliberal globalization as measured in the growing poverty and environmental damage in many regions of the developing world. In seeking social justice and environmental sustainability, however, fair trade pursues a market-based solution to the very problems developing from free markets.[26]

They go on to make an even more damning claim: "In place of legal and policy remedies by states on behalf of the farmers and workers who reside within their borders, fair trade seeks social justice by embracing the deregulated markets that are themselves often responsible for deepening poverty in rural communities."

Although many people inside the movement denounced capitalism, neoliberalism and deregulation, they are promoting a movement that works within this same system. I am not arguing here that this view is hypocritical, as many fair-trade promoters are self-consciously working within the system but also advocating for structural changes to improve the living conditions of producers around the globe. The problem, as I see it, is that fair traders are creating a sharp moral boundary around their movement, likely discouraging participation by the very segments of the population whose engagement might well lead to more material surpluses for producers.

If fair trade continues to be associated with upper-class, cosmopolitan consumers, it may continue to act as a form of symbolic violence among consumers who do not possess the requisite cultural capital to understand the value of fair trade. (For example, Dunkin' Donuts is conscious of this issue and therefore avoids overtly publicizing the fact that its espresso drinks are made from fair-trade coffee).[27] This conundrum is not simply an academic exercise for those interested in cultural studies. It is a fiercely contested debate playing out within a range of consumer-dependent movements right now.

Consumer-dependent movements for social change need to attract a large number of shoppers to raise funds for charitable causes. But, in reaching a mass audience, fair-trade products tend to lose their distinctiveness, failing to attach the stories of producers that are the basis for the growth of the movement. In essence, this cat-and-mouse game within fair trade is detrimental to the future growth of the movement. As fair trade goes mainstream, it loses the support of the promoters who are so essential to the moral integrity of the movement. But the mainstreaming of fair trade is essential to provide market access and an improved quality of life for artisans and farmers. The drawing and redrawing of these symbolic boundaries has important repercussions for the meaning of fair trade and the material surpluses for producers.

Shopping is greatly influenced by market forces. Friedrich Engels famously argued that our morality is shaped by our economic class position.[28] While we can debate the extent to which our moral behavior is influenced by economic factors, there is no doubt that our economic standing has some influence on our moral views. Michele Micheletti and Andreas Follesdal seem to agree; as they ominously wrote before the beginning of the Great Recession, "If people have less or no money to invest and corporations start to economize, capitalism may once again become focused on the relationship between price and material quality rather than the social connections embedded in economic transactions."[29] I suspect that Micheletti and Follesdal may be correct.

There is historical precedent for economic changes influencing Americans' views on the morality of shopping. Ellen Ruppel Shell explains that in the middle of the twentieth century, discount shopping was stigmatized among the middle and upper classes. With the introduction of the credit card in 1949 and an increased desire to "keep up with the Joneses," this stigma began to loosen:

> Middle-class consumers who wanted a showy car or a boat or a trip to Paris saved for these luxuries by cutting corners where they could on commodities such as children's clothes, toiletries, hardware, and even food. As more and more respectable people sought low price, discount shopping lost its stigma. It would gradually become the norm.[30]

Although I am unable to prove it, I suspect that the Great Recession also affected consumers' shared meanings of shopping. With the country's unemployment rate hovering around 10 percent in October of 2009, I believe that the stigma conscientious consumers attached to shopping at places like Walmart was reduced. In a time of great economic prosperity, it seems logical for highly educated, cosmopolitan consumers (promoters and conscientious consumers) to criticize shoppers who are concerned mostly about prices. But when cultural norms shift, as they did following this crisis (for example, consumers began saving at higher rates), it seems logical that they would be less likely to criticize retailers that focus strongly on prices. This change in meaning seems like a logical outcome of significant economic decline.

On the other hand, there are some hints that the Great Recession did not impact all fair-trade initiatives equally. Upon returning to my field sites following the Great Recession, I could not help thinking that Ten Thousand Villages was better positioned to deal with the economic crisis than the coffee shops. Managers at Ten Thousand Villages encourage every employee to tell stories about the handicrafts to each customer who enters the store. Yes, many consumers are uninterested, but others like to hear the stories, and a few even quickly "buy into" the fair-trade philosophy. The greater emphasis on storytelling likely created more value for these products in the eyes of consumers than their daily coffee ritual, which I often found to be devoid of fair-trade narratives. Additionally, Ten Thousand Villages relies heavily on volunteer labor, and this protected the organization from the slight decrease in sales during the recession.

Possibilities of Shopping for Change

Buying into fair trade allows consumers to recreate their identities. Whereas the de-emphasis on storytelling prevents some consumers from thinking critically about their purchases, for others, socially responsible shopping is a way to remake their own identities. Whether it's boycotting chain stores or giving gifts of hand-carved, fair-trade onyx from Pakistan, some consumers derive great meaning from shopping for fair-trade products. Although this type of shopping does carry the risk of duping consumers into thinking they are making significant changes in the world, it may also encourage them to think more critically about all of their purchases. Perhaps the fetishization of fair trade has a silver lining?

This is the argument that Juliet Schor, a professor of sociology at Boston College, makes in her most recent book, *Plenitude*.[31] In a creative twist on conventional ways of thinking about ethical consumption, Schor argues that if consumers are serious about improving the environment, they need to become more materialistic, not less.[32] If consumers start thinking more about where the stuff they buy comes from, who made it, and how those producers benefit, then the products will become more valuable. In other words, American consumers are not materialistic enough. Yes, we are buying more clothes, sofas, electronics, handicrafts, and coffee than ever before. And this is a problem. The mass production, shipment, and disposal of these goods are contributing to an environmental disaster. But if we begin to care more about the cultural biographies of these products, we will likely treat them as sacred objects, objects we would not want to quickly throw away.

The fair-trade movement opens the window for a more materialistic relationship between our products and ourselves. Handicraft retailers include detailed stories about all the products they sell, and coffee retailers display advertisements of smiling, presumably empowered farmers throughout their cafés. Nevertheless, the extent to which fair trade is actually opening a dialogue with consumers is an open question, which Juliet Schor and Margaret Willis are beginning to answer.[33] They are trying to uncover the extent to which socially responsible consumption can act as a "gateway drug" to a life of activism. There is some evidence that this is, in fact, occurring.

Michael Shellenberger conducted focus groups with Home Depot consumers shopping in the Eco Option aisle of the store. Working for an environmental research firm, he was surprised at his findings:

> We didn't find that people felt that their consumption gave them a pass, so to speak. . . . They knew what they were doing wasn't going to deal with the problems, and these little consumer things won't add up. But they do it as a practice of mindfulness. They didn't see it as antithetical to political action. Folks who were engaged in these green practices were actually becoming more committed to more transformative political action on global warming.[34]

Instead of giving them "license" to shop in a more exploitative fashion, these customers hinted that eco-friendly shopping was part of a transformative process in creating a more socially conscious consumer.

Although there are strong opinions about the potential of fair trade to remake the world, we need more research into the relationship between consumption and our identities, worldviews, and support for social justice. Can shopping ethically lead to other forms of activism? Can it inspire hope? Can it lead to a different way of thinking about global citizenship? I hope that future scholars will look for patterns of sustainable consumption across countries. Understanding why the market for fair trade and other socially conscious products is so much more robust in Europe than in the United States may contribute to our understandings about America itself. Cross-cultural research on socially responsible consumption will provide a promising window to understand how meaning making is conducted at the point of purchase.

Altruistic shopping can change farmers' and artisans' lives. Although I have been critical throughout this book of the mismatch between the claims of fair-trade promoters and the actual benefits of fair trade for farmers and artisans, it is worth reiterating that fair trade does have a positive impact on many producers' lives. Fair Trade USA estimates that fair-trade premiums from sales in the United States between 1998 and 2009 have returned about $220 million to coffee farmers.[35] On a smaller scale, consumers of Independents coffee houses in Philly helped a group of farmers install solar dryers for their coffee beans at a total cost of $12,000. (Admittedly, however, it is unclear how many consumers were even aware that their purchases went to this cause!) Yes, I think we should remain critical of these initiatives to shop for a cause. We will never be able to shop our way out of the huge social problems associated with overconsumption.[36] Nevertheless, if we are going to continue to shop, we can do it in a better way.

The rifts between the mission and the movement wing of the fair-trade effort are real and will determine the future of the movement. Importantly, however, both wings of the movement share common goals about improving the lives of coffee farmers. They just differ on the best ways to accomplish these goals. It behooves many in the movement to step back and focus more on the benefits being returned to artisans and farmers, rather than paying too much attention to cultural positioning for status within fair-trade markets.

Conclusion

In *Buying into Fair Trade*, I have sought to understand the ways conscientious consumers make sense of the world around them. I wanted to uncover the ways they confront the moral hazards of shopping ethically, without letting my criticisms of their actions guide this story. In essence, I wanted to avoid falling into the trap of moralizing about consumer culture. As Daniel Miller writes:

> The discrepancy between the quantity and the quality of [consumer] research is largely a result of the central role taken by morality within consumption research which has led to this branch of studies becoming largely a site where academics can demonstrate their stance towards the world, rather than a place where the world stands as a potential empirical critique of our assumptions about it.[37]

In interviewing a wide range of fair-trade consumers, I was struck by the level of reflexivity they demonstrated toward their ethical shopping initiatives. I agree with Miller as he continues his critique of conventional scholarship:

> Far from expressing capitalism, consumption is most commonly used by people to negate it. To merely critique it as the creature of capitalism is therefore to ignore the practice of actual consumers. But the moralists who need to use consumption for their critique of capitalism cannot understand that for ordinary people consumption is actually the way that they confront, on a day-to-day basis, their sense of alienation.[38]

This sentiment was expressed best during one of my first interviews with Sarah, a fair-trade promoter and co-owner of an Independents café. Sarah remembers fondly the time she began to tell friends and family that she was starting a business that would judge success according to a triple bottom line of people, planet, and profits. She told me that some people thought she was "crazy." They would tell her, "You know, we're not Europe. We're not a socialist country. We'll never be Sweden. We can't do that, we'll never have universal health care." The comments always stung, but Sarah said she responded by asking herself:

> Why not? If we're all-powerful and all-mighty and can do all of these great things, then don't tell me we can't do it. Because you can say where there's a will there's a way. We'd figure it out if we really wanted to. And we figured out how to do it on a much smaller scale. But I would share our business model with anybody that wanted to try to replicate it or improve upon it. Certainly we're not perfect. There's certainly areas where we could improve.

Sarah's relentless optimism was and continues to be inspiring. Yes, there is much to be critical about within fair trade. Sarah is aware of most of these criticisms but feels she has to strive to make the world a better place. I found similar inspiration from many of my interactions with promoters.

The growth and future direction of the fair-trade movement is driven by a relatively small segment of influential individuals like Sarah. Most are store owners, consumer activists, and NGO employees, many of whom have participated in emotionally intense experiences while traveling abroad to meet with fair-trade artisans and farmers. These travel experiences, combined with interactions with fair-trade artisans and farmers traveling to the United States, serve to motivate continued participation in the fair-trade movement. Ultimately, becoming embedded in networks of like-minded individuals (think store owners who are constantly talking about fair trade) plays a significant role in sustaining individuals' identities as supporters of fair trade. Equally important, seeing with their own eyes how fair trade aids coffee farmers lends credibility and authenticity to the stories that promoters tell about fair trade.

When the promoters come back to the United States with evocative tales about life in the *campo*, they quickly realize that there is a distinct time and place to tell these types of stories. More often than not, they avoid moral distinctions in their conversations with people who know little or nothing about fair trade. They often avoid telling others how they "ought to" consume and focus on issues such as product attributes (e.g., price, aesthetics, quality) when trying to convince people to shop ethically. In essence, they still want others to shop responsibly, but they stress socially responsible consumption in a calculated fashion. This avoidance of moral issues is an attempt to evade discussions that could be viewed as "too preachy" by others.

Research Methods

I was never a coffee drinker. I entered a coffee shop only two or three times before starting graduate school in 2000. They made me uncomfortable. I didn't like the taste of coffee, and I didn't even know what to call many of the pastries on display. I also knew almost nothing about handicrafts before starting this project. The French sociologist Pierre Bourdieu would probably say that I did not possess the requisite "cultural capital" to feel comfortable in these environments. If nothing else, graduate school provides students with cultural capital. Besides learning how to fix copy machines, graduate students learn how to interact in diverse environments, eat a wider array of foods, and consume a wider array of arts and culture. And this is exactly what happened to me.

While conducting research for this book, I transitioned from an outsider to an insider within the fair-trade community. I started drinking coffee. I learned how to brew it properly, how to distinguish between high- and low-quality coffee, and how to talk about the benefits of fair trade for artisans. I provide this information because I think it is important to explain where I fit into the fair-trade world. All research, but ethnographic research in particular, is interpretive. The stories in this book are told from my perspective. I tried to think about my interactions with fair traders from an array of different vantage points. I wanted to understand the motives behind consumer discourse and action, but I also wanted to be critical of the viewpoints expressed by many of the people I observed and interviewed. I wanted to try to understand when interviewees were being honest and when they were trying to present themselves in a positive light.

In essence, I was trying to capture individuals' "lived" or subjective experiences within the fair-trade world and, at the same time, map those perspectives into a broader, objective space.[1] I was attempting to understand how socially responsible entrepreneurs, consumers, and activists think about markets and how they position themselves in relation to others within those markets. Throughout this project, my goal was to provide an understanding of the sociocultural forces that encourage individuals to seek out fair-trade and other ethically produced products. I wanted to understand how individuals use commodities as a bridge and a barrier in their interactions with others. And I wanted to understand how individuals' everyday purchases serve as a window into how they view an increasingly global world. I believe the stories, interviews, and interactions described in this book do just that.

Coffee and Handicrafts

Selecting coffee and handicrafts for this research allowed me to see a bit of variation within the fair trade marketplace. I believed that the differences between these two products would offer some insight into how individuals make sense of ethical consumption. This proved to be the case, as both of these products are framed in very different ways. The emphasis on storytelling at Ten Thousand Villages is much more profound than in any of the coffee shops I visited. Handicrafts are more often given as gifts than is coffee and are also more expensive. Coffee was a part of many individuals' daily ritual. They frequented the same shops every day or a few times a week. As a result, café employees did not feel compelled to tell a fair-trade story to these customers each time they interacted. Through observations and interviews at both Ten Thousand Villages and the Independents cafés, I soon learned that consumers were reluctant to talk about fair-trade initiatives and instead chose to deflect attention onto other issues.

I volunteered at a Ten Thousand Villages inside Philadelphia's city boundary. I worked four hours one day a week from July 2005 until December 2006. As a volunteer, I spent time unpacking boxes, cleaning the store, going to make deposits at the bank, restocking the shelves, and serving customers. I worked during the bustling holiday season and during the slow, hot August months. I was able to collect ethnographic data on what consumers were "doing" (rather than "saying") about fair trade. I was able to examine the extent to which they were buying into the fair-trade philosophy and the extent to which they cared more about finding handicrafts that would make a good gift or match the furniture.

I told the local store manager about my research and also spoke with upper-level managers who also gave me permission to collect data. I was surprised at the level of access that I was given. I was allowed to attend the annual training workshop for store managers, where I collected rich data and great insight into the goals of Ten Thousand Villages. I was also given marketing information about "Gwen" that I used as the introduction to chapter 4. One of the goals to which many organizations within fair trade claim to strive is transparency. Ten Thousand Villages was remarkably open and honest with me throughout this project. To its staff, I am incredibly grateful.

In addition to volunteering at Ten Thousand Villages, I spent three to four days per week between 2005 and 2008 hanging out at the four original Independents coffee houses: the Greenline (West Philadelphia), Infusion Coffee and Tea (Mount Airy), Joe Coffee Bar (Center City), and Mugshots Coffee House and Café (Fairmount). The neighborhoods in which these shops were located greatly impacted their economic success and struggles. Stores that tended to be more successful were in neighborhoods that had few other coffee shops nearby, attracted highly educated consumers, and were in residential neighborhoods. Informally, all of the coffee-shop owners said that location was one of the most important determinants of a café's success.

I examined how these stores were laid out, how the coffee was promoted in advertisements, and how retail staff talked about fair trade with their customers. In the coffee shops, most owners chose to emphasize that they were not like Starbucks and were independently owned, rather than talking a lot about fair-trade coffee. Very few customers talked about fair trade while at these coffee shops. Understanding how people were acting within these coffee shops influenced the types of questions I asked while interviewing consumers, store owners, and fair-trade advocates.

Seven store owners of four coffee shops founded the Independents Coffee Cooperative, which was designed to help independently owned shops purchase products in bulk and to jointly promote the stores that participated in the cooperative. Independents also provided technical assistance and training to new members of the cooperative on how to

best train staff, how to best clean coffee pots, how to deal with graduate students who camp out all day in the shop without spending much
money, and so on. The members prided themselves on promoting socially responsible goods such as fair-trade coffee, locally produced and
organic foods, and environmentally responsible products. The first four
shops in the cooperative, which were founded by the original members
of the cooperative, are described in the following paragraphs.

Joe Coffee Bar was the first fair-trade coffee shop to open in Philadelphia. The store was located in Center City Philadelphia, on 11th and
Walnut Streets. The store benefited from its location on Thomas Jeffer-
son University's campus. Doctors, medical students, and local activist
groups often frequented the store. The store sold coffee, tea, local and
organic foods, and imported Italian coffee accessories. Joe's café was
located right next to the Forrest Theater, which brought in a lot of additional business for the three to four shows performed there each year.
Joe's was not located in a residential neighborhood, and its business suffered on the weekends, when people had to travel a farther distance to
frequent the store. While Joe Coffee Bar was located at a busy intersec-
tion, the store was set far back off the sidewalk and was a little hard to
notice from the street. The inside of the store had very high ceilings, a
mannequin in the middle of the store, and colorful tables. There were
windows on two sides of the store. Joe reserved two walls of the café for
local photographers and artists to present their work for one month at
a time. After Hurricane Katrina hit, the proceeds from one photogra-
pher's work were donated to the American Red Cross.

The Green Line Café opened in January 2003. The owners purchased the
building at 43nd and Baltimore in West Philadelphia and are the only
members of Independents who pay a mortgage rather than rent. The
Green Line is located in a residential neighborhood made up of many
students, activists, and employees of the University of Pennsylvania.
The owners bought the store before the University of Pennsylvania announced an initiative to promote growth in West Philadelphia by subsi-
dizing home loans for university employees. This initiative has sparked
a lot of gentrification in the area, causing further tensions between local
peoples and the often transient populations that attend the university.

Nevertheless, the initiative has also sparked an increase in development in West Philadelphia; a local paper compared the change to the resurgence of Center City Philadelphia that occurred in the late 1990s and early 2000s.

The Greenline Café is a brightly lit corner store with two large windows looking out over Clark Park. The park itself is a community gathering place where people take their kids sledding, walk their dogs, and host picnics. The store was intentionally created to contrast with the design of Starbucks stores and to promote interactions among community members. The colors of the walls were even chosen so that they did not resemble the pale yellow used in many Starbucks in the mid-2000s. The owners do not provide wireless Internet access because they want to promote more face-to-face interactions among customers. The store is almost always filled with students typing on computers and local residents meeting for a cup of coffee. Local artists perform music and show their paintings on the walls of the Greenline Café. Since it first opened, the store has been very successful and has allowed the owners to open two other coffee shops in West Philadelphia.

Mugshots Coffeehouse and Café is currently located at 1925 Fairmount Ave. in the Art Museum section of Philadelphia. It was originally located on the corner of 21st and Fairmount Ave. Mugshots was named in reference to the Philadelphia Eastern State Penitentiary, which is located across the street. Eastern State Penitentiary no longer houses inmates but has become a prominent tourist destination, especially during Halloween, when it conducts haunted-house tours of the prison. Mugshots provides the most extensive food menu of any of the Independents shops, offering local, organic, and free-range meals. Meals such as the "Capone" and the "Slammer" play off the prison theme. The store has been well received by the local community and is often filled to capacity. The owners put up "no camping" signs on the tables as they try to discourage students and other working professionals from occupying the tables for long periods while only ordering one or two drinks. Like West Philadelphia, the Art Museum area is experiencing the frictions associated with gentrification.

Mugshots is characterized by exposed brick walls and photographs and paintings by local artists. The store regularly shows independent and cult movies. The owners of Mugshots opened a second store in Manayunk, a third store in the Brewerytown section of Philadelphia, and a fourth store on Temple University's campus. The store in Manayunk shut down in the fall of 2011.

InFusion, a coffee and tea gallery was opened in December 2002 by a married couple who grew up in the Philadelphia area. They were traveling together throughout Southeast Asia when they realized they wanted to open a local coffee shop that could incorporate their values. InFusion sells fair-trade coffee, vegan desserts, and organic and locally made meals. The store is located at 7133 Germantown Avenue in Mount Airy, a racially and economically diverse residential area in Northwest Philadelphia. The store has a large table where students are often found typing on their laptops, a comfortable set of couches, plush chairs, and an area for children to hang out and play. There is a large desk in the café that is designed to get people to interact with one another. The store benefits from a large outdoor patio that greatly increases the number of people who can be in the store at one time. The owners also post local artwork and provide a large library where customers can pick out books to browse.

Ethnographic Data

Ethnography refers to the systematic study of culture. Whereas interviews allow researchers to understand how individuals talk about issues and position themselves in relation to others, ethnography allows researchers to see how people actually behave. Each time I entered a field site (e.g., a coffeehouse, trip to Nicaragua), I took extensive descriptive field notes. I tried to be as detailed as possible. I made great efforts to reconstruct exactly what people were saying during our interactions. When I was certain of a direct quotation, I included the statement in quotation marks. When I was uncertain, I avoided using quotation marks. This is the guideline I used for quotations throughout this book. I entered and analyzed all of my field notes in NVivo, a qualitative software analysis program.

I collected data at many "extended field sites" for this book. I describe many of these sites briefly in chapter 1, but it is worth explaining a little bit more about my trip to Nicaragua. I traveled to Nicaragua to learn more about the people who go on "reality tours" to developing countries. I wanted to understand what motivates participation in these trips, what types of stories participants tell upon returning home, and how it feels to experience a reality tour. I took extensive field notes throughout the ten-day trip. Often I took notes in the middle of the day. I stayed up late each night writing down as much as I could remember. I also stayed in contact with the other travelers. I did not, however, describe the high school students who attended this trip in much detail. I also did not follow up with them after returning home. My Institutional Review Board application did not permit me to interview individuals under eighteen, and I did not realize that these students would be on the trip until I arrived in Nicaragua. I conducted face-to-face interviews with three of the other participants in Massachusetts after we returned home. And I conducted phone interviews with almost everyone else. All of these interviews took place between one and three months after the end of the trip.

Interviews

In total, I conducted formal interviews with 103 customers, store owners and managers, consumer advocates, and members of fair trade nongovernmental organizations. Although most people who I met wore multiple hats within the fair-trade movement, fifty-three identified primarily as consumers, twenty-five as owners, managers, or volunteers, and twenty-five as activists or NGO employees working primarily on fair-trade campaigns.

The Fair Trade Research Network (FTRN) hired me to conduct twenty-seven of these interviews as part of a project whose goal was to assess the current state and the future direction of the fair-trade movement. I helped design an interview guide and provided basic interview training for the other three researchers who helped conduct these interviews. Almost all of these interviews were conducted over the phone, and most lasted between twenty-five and forty-five minutes. Each interviewer took detailed notes while conducting the interview. I analyzed the reoccurring themes in these interviews and helped put together a presentation for a Fair Trade Futures conference in Baltimore,

Maryland, in May 2006. Between twenty and thirty national leaders of the fair-trade movement attended the conference (most were interviewed). These respondents all agreed to let me use their interviews for this research project.

I included a few questions in the interview guide about the reasons these individuals (all promoters) decided to enter the fair-trade movement. I would not have been able to get insight about national leaders of fair trade without working with the FTRN. Additionally, collecting data and attending this conference allowed me to see how insiders think about fair trade. Their concerns about proper ethical sourcing of coffee were very different from the concerns of consumers, who were willing to simply trust that their local shop provided high-quality and ethically sourced coffee. The mission-versus-market tensions within fair trade became apparent during this conference. I am not sure I would have been able to understand how fair-trade companies and nonprofit organizations distinguish themselves from their peers if I had not attended this conference.

Admittedly, however, the telephone interviews that we conducted were not as rich as the face-to-face interviews I conducted with all my other interviewees. With only notes from each interview (as opposed to a recording), it was tough to grasp some of the more subtle nuanced meanings of these interviews. I conducted the remaining seventy-six interviews with consumers, store owners, activists, and store managers in Philadelphia. I approached consumers while volunteering at Ten Thousand Villages and while sitting in the four original Independents cafés. I was surprised that the great majority of people I approached agreed to an interview. In each instance, we scheduled another time and place to meet. I conducted interviews in people's homes and at workplaces, organic grocery stores, train stations, Indian restaurants, Starbucks, and independently owned coffee shops. Some of the people that I approached knew little or nothing about fair trade. In all but two instances, I decided not to interview these individuals. The names of all but one of the interviewees (Joe Cesa) have been changed to protect their identities.

I intended to hide the identities of all the people who spoke to me for this project as best I could. If I used a person's real name, I included his or her last name and took the quotation from a public source (newspaper or conference with Paul Rice). Many of the people in Philadelphia's fair-trade community know one another, and café owners would have been quick to identify Joe even if I had changed his name. While working on this book, I shared earlier drafts of these chapters with some of the promoters about whom I talk in this book. I shared descriptions of them that were sometimes critical of the ways they talked or behaved. Since Joe was featured so prominently, he asked if I could use his real name, and I agreed. In the notes to chapter 2, Joe responds to a few of my more critical descriptions of him.

Most interviews lasted between one and two hours. All of them were tape recorded and transcribed. I entered all the transcripts into NVivo. I used this program to code for dominant trends that I saw while gathering data. (I include the coding sheet I used for this project at the end of this appendix.) The coding sheet helped me to look at the ways conscientious consumers and promoters talk about moral issues; the codes helped me look at interview and ethnographic data about when people felt comfortable enacting strong moral boundaries (how people "should" behave or shop) and when they avoided these types of issues.

Before each interview, I asked all my respondents to fill out a calendar listing all of the places they had shopped in the previous week. I made sure to stress that shopping can be broadly defined to include such items and places as groceries, clothes, snacks, drinks, malls, gas stations, convenience stores, farmers markets, coffee shops, video rentals, and places where they bought breakfast, lunch, or dinner. My goal was to get respondents to think about the wide variety of places where they spend money. Although all respondents signed a consent form that explained the goals of the project, many still seemed a bit uncertain about the direction of the interviews. This ended up being very helpful, as I do not think that individuals were trying to position themselves as a certain "type" of consumer (socially conscious) when filling out this shopping worksheet. Although I did not systematically code these calendars to see exactly what types of stores people were shopping at, the calendars did prove to be helpful. Many individuals referred to the calendars during the interview. And I occasionally used the calendars as a prompt during the interview, asking whether interviewees viewed certain stores and products as ethical. For instance, when individuals said something that suggested that they were trying to simply appear to be conscientious consumers, I asked them how they had thought about sustainability and ethics issues last Wednesday when they were shopping at CVS. Often, these somewhat more conflictual interactions led to conversations that seemed particularly genuine and sincere.

Consumer Interview Guide

CONSUMPTION
Do you have any favorite stores to shop at?
    What do you like about these stores?
Are there any stores you really dislike?
    What do you dislike about these stores?
Who does most of the shopping in your household?
When you go shopping, do you go alone?
What are the criteria for a "good buy" or a "great deal"?

HANDICRAFTS ADDITION
Do you shop online?
Do you read any magazines or newspapers? Which ones?
Do you visit any websites frequently?

CLUBS/ORGANIZATIONS/SOCIAL MOVEMENTS/HOBBIES
Have you had much experience traveling? Where have you traveled? (international/national)
Are you a member of any clubs/organizations? (political, economic, work related)
Have you participated in any recent social movements or protests? (probe for types of movements—Iraq war, race/gender based movements)
What do you think about unions?

FAIR TRADE
Do you ever think about where the stuff you buy comes from?
Do you ever think about the people who made all the stuff you buy?
How often do you shop at _____? (coffee or handicraft shop recruited from)
    How often do you purchase FT products? (coffee, handicrafts, etc.)

Why do you shop at _____? (coffee or handicraft shop recruited from)

What does fair trade mean to you?

How did you first learn about FT?

Do you have any friends who also like to purchase FT goods?

Have you ever given a FT product as a gift?

    Describe the experience. Did you tell them it was a FT product?

    How did the person respond?

Do you consider yourself a part of the FT movement?

What kind of a difference can the FT movement make?

    How do you think about FT—as a movement, a market, or both?

Do you have trust in the label "Fair Trade"?

Show various FT labels to the interviewee and see if they are recognizable

    (TransFair USA, new international FT symbol, Equal Exchange logo).

GENERAL QUESTIONS

What are the three biggest problems facing society today?

    Can these problems be resolved? How?

How would you describe yourself? (three characteristics)

BIOGRAPHICAL INFORMATION

Racial identification

Where were you born? Where did you grow up?

Where did you go to school? (high school, college, other)

Where do you work?

What did your parents (guardians) do for a living? (father, mother)

    Parents' education

What are your most recent jobs? (past and current jobs)

Do you have any hobbies? (probe about other interests)

What is your household income per year?

Coding Sheet

LIVED DEMOGRAPHICS AND IDENTITY ISSUES

Gender Issues: Any discussion or issue that indicates gender differences or gendered interactions. Also includes dialogue where a probing question should have been asked about issues dealing with gender.

Racial Issues: Products that in any way can be linked to racial issues, whether racialized interactions, marketing that targets or exploits racial or ethnic identities, or even expressions of "ethnic goods" desired by certain groups of people.

Class Issues: Class-based issues that are either explicitly or implicitly discussed. Wide range of issues accepted, from interactions, marketing, discussions of wealth, etc.

Age: Any discussions around age and how it is important or not for the consumption of fair-trade handicrafts.

Religion: Any discussion of religious affiliation or importance of religion on consumption, worldly perspectives, or activities.

Not a Shopper: Any discussion about not identifying as a big shopper or resistance to being labeled as such.

Shopper: Any discussion indicating that the interviewee considers themselves to be big shoppers or greatly enjoys shopping. Also code language around the joys and pleasures derived from shopping.

POLITICAL AND ETHICAL CONSUMPTION

Moral Boundaries: Any discussions of differences or distinctions based on ethics, morals, or doing the "right thing."

Purity: Any discussion using "purity" or related words as they relate to consumption. The search for the most pure products.

Authenticity: Any discussion involving the search for authenticity. This code also includes discussions about products being handmade.

Politics: Any discussion of formal politics or policies, particularly as they relate to consumption.

Social Movements: Any discussion of social movement participation, broadly conceived.

Antisweatshop: Any discussion of the antisweatshop movement or sweatshop issues.

Antichain Sentiments: Any discussion either pros or cons dealing with chain stores or restaurants.

Boycotts: Any discussion about consumer boycotts.

Globalization: Any emphasis on global issues, liberally coded to include discussions of local issues as they are related to global conditions or changes.

Unions: Any discussion involving unions, broadly conceived.

Children: Any discussion of constraints or possibilities opened up because of children as they relate to consumption.

Big Corporations: Walmart/Nike/Starbucks/etc., any discussion of these topics.

GENERAL CONSUMPTION ISSUES

Therapeutic Consumption: Any discussion about consuming in order to feel better about one's self.

Guilt: Any discussion of guilt as it relates to shopping or consumption.

Status: Cultural distinctions based on the production or consumption of fair-trade products.

Emotions: Any links to emotions. Emotional resonance, emotions dealing with IFAT logo, emotions upon returning home from trips.

Money: Discussions around money, liberally coded.

Contradictions: Any discussion where the interviewee contradicts himself or herself either knowingly or unknowingly.

Trust: Issues related to trust, either a lack of trust of fair-trade certification or a lack of trust of the motives for corporations.

FAIR TRADE

Definition of Fair Trade: How fair trade is defined and explained to other people.

Health Issues: Any discussion about health issues, healthy living, or reasons for beginning to buy fair trade. Chemical sensitivity and eating organic because it is more healthy are especially key.

Movement and Market Tensions: Discussions about movement and market tensions in lived experiences.

Pathways to Fair Trade: Discussions about how people first learned about fair trade.

Certification Organizations: Any discussion about TransFair, FLO, IFAT, or any other certification organization.

Gift Giving: Any discussion about the exchange of fair-trade gifts.

Little to No Awareness: Interviewee expresses little to no awareness about fair trade. Clear misinformation should also be coded.

Aesthetics: Emphasis on the aesthetic properties of commodities.

Taste: Any discussion about the taste of a fair trade or socially responsible product.

ARS (*Alternative Reward Structure*): Any discussion of alternative rewards or alternative motivations (other than profit) for continued fair-trade participation.

NOTES

CHAPTER 1

1. DeCarlo 2007.
2. Global Exchange 2012.
3. Osorio 2002.
4. Smith 2010, p. 31.
5. Jaffee 2007; DeCarlo 2007; Lyon 2011.
6. Gould (1993) theorized that social movement participation is determined in part by individuals' belief that their actions in support of a movement will efficiently go towards a social problem. These trips foster this belief. This idea is explored in more depth in chapter 3.
7. Giddens 2000.
8. Smith and Johnston 2002; Klein 2001.
9. Kimeldorf et al. 2006.
10. The research on fair trade is growing quickly. A dynamic database keeping track of the latest research on the fair trade movement can be found at www.fairtrade-institute.org/.
11. DeCarlo 2007.
12. DeCarlo 2007, p. 67.
13. Jaffee 2007, p. 12; DeCarlo 2007.
14. Akerloff and Kranton 2010, p. 41.
15. Bryant Simon (2009) makes this point with the title of his book about Starbucks, attributing the company's success to "Everything but the coffee." Gary Alan Fine (2003, 2004) shows that the stories about a piece of art are often more important than the object itself. The value of self-taught art (sometimes referred to as outsider art) is largely determined by the authenticity of the stories associated with the artist. Pierre Bourdieu (1984) explains that individuals are searching for distinction and thus attach certain meanings to certain products. These meanings tend to be related to a person's economic position and level of cultural capital. Holt clarifies Bourdieu's point by explaining that it is not just consumption that reflects social status; it is the way in which individuals talk about the products they buy. The stories describing why individuals chose a certain home or vacation serve to convey a person's class position and how much cultural capital a person possesses (Holt 2000).
16. I compiled this number by comparing the number of international trips (not including Mexico or Canada) taken by Americans in 1988, which came to

approximately 14.4 million trips (International Trade Administration 1998) with the number of trips taken in 2010, which totaled about 28.5 million trips (International Trade Administration 2010). The total number of trips decreased by 5.9 percent between 2009 and 2010.

17. Economists have even begun to alter their conventional models in order to catch up with these types of market exchanges. George Akerloff and Rachel Kranton (2010) explain that identity, culture, and contexts all greatly influence economic transactions.

18. Equal Exchange 2011.

19. Tarmann 2002; Paige 1997.

20. Pendergrast 2010.

21. Lyon 2011.

22. Coffee trees take from three to five years before the cherries can be harvested. Brazil recovered just as many other countries began to increase their coffee production.

23. Talbot 2004.

24. International Coffee Organization 2012.

25. The recent coffee crisis raised awareness about the plight of global coffee farmers, but coffee has a long history of boom-bust cycles that extends back to the late nineteenth century. Mark Pendergrast (2010, p. xxi), author of *Uncommon Grounds: The History of Coffee and How It Transformed Our World*, writes that the recent crisis "was not a surprise" and that this boom-bust cycle "will continue in the future, unless we somehow learn more from the distant and recent past."

26. Weissman 2008.

27. Pendergrast 2010.

28. Ritzer 2011.

29. Simon 2009.

30. Pendergrast 2010; Weissman 2008.

31. Weissman 2008.

32. Fair Trade USA 2011a.

33. Raynolds 2002; Lyon 2011.

34. Lyon 2011.

35. Jaffee (2007) shows that some of these coyotes are also farmers and, at least in some instances, are also not aware of the international price of coffee.

36. Lyon and Moberg 2010.

37. Brown 2008. In *The Field of Cultural Production* (1993, p. 39), Pierre Bourdieu argues that all markets are organized by a similar tension among producers who "produce for other producers" and producers who produce for a mass audience. Within fair trade, the mission-driven wing of the movement represents the former, and the more profit-oriented wing represents the latter.

38. Fair Trade USA 2010.

39. Fair Trade Research Network 2011.
40. Robinson 2011.
41. Solidarity eXchange 2011.
42. Rice 2012.
43. United Students for Fair Trade 2011.
44. Bryant Simon (2010) estimates that at least one-quarter of Starbucks' signage discusses its fair-trade coffee. Further, the signage varies significantly by location. In Japan, there are few signs promoting fair-trade coffee, whereas, in the United Kingdom, the signs are all over the place. In the United States, there tend to be more fair-trade signs in Starbucks stores located close to college campuses.
45. Jaffee 2007.
46. Moberg and Lyon 2010, pp. 11–12.
47. CAN 2011.
48. Fairtrade Labeling Organizations Association 2011. It is important to reiterate that Fair Trade USA and FLO certify many products, but coffee is currently driving the growth of the fair trade movement. The rift between FLO and Fair Trade USA presents a threat to the well-being of coffee farmers and the gains made by fair trade entrepreneurs who want consumers to understand what fair trade certification means.
49. United Students for Fair Trade 2011.
50. Moberg and Lyon 2010.
51. White 2002; Bourdieu 1984.
52. A quick note about my use of "ethical," "moral," and "altruistic" is warranted. I tend to use these phrases interchangeably throughout the book. I argue not that products are inherently moral or ethical but that consumers view them as such. They view fair-trade coffee, for instance, as better or more socially conscious than conventional coffee.
53. King 2006.
54. Micheletti and Follesdal 2007.
55. Matathia and Salzman 1999.
56. A line of products also referred to as Product RED, RED, or (RED). These labels are often combined with product and brand names in a variety of different ways. See Richey and Ponte 2011
57. Cohen 2003.
58. Cohen 2003, p. 31.
59. Cohen 2003, pp. 18–19.
60. Goodman (2004) characterizes this type of social movement as "consumer-dependent" rather than "consumer-driven." I think this distinction is important because it's not so much the consumers who are driving change in the fair trade market but the "promoters," who are often coffee roasters, advocates, retailers, or members of nongovernmental organizations. This was made clear to me when "conscientious consumers" told me they sought fair-trade coffee because they

trust the owner of their local café. Many consumers had little knowledge about what fair trade means, but they felt it was a "better" way to purchase coffee.

61. Here are just a few: http://www.carbonfootprint.com/calculator.aspx; http://terrapass.com/carbon-footprint-calculator.

62. Schor 2010.

63. Schor 2010.

64. SC Johnson and Son settled a lawsuit for creating a confusing label certifying that Windex was a "green" product. The label hinted that Windex was certified by a third-party (PR Newswire 2011). Similarly, Starbucks has its own CAFÉ practices that are designed to ensure sustainability.

65. Veblen [1899] 1953.

66. See Binkley 2003.

67. Bourdieu 1993.

68. Gladwell 2000.

69. Livestrong 2012.

70. Walker 2008.

71. Taylor 2006.

72. Schneider 2004.

73. Griskevicius et al. 2010.

74. Norris 2008. I am arguing that the lower prices allow consumers to feel that they are saving money. But, as economists are quick to point out, this does not necessarily mean that environmentally friendly advantages will come from this change in consumer behavior. William Stanley Jevons found that improvements in coal technology led to increased uses of energy. This "Jevons paradox" or rebound effect occurs when technological improvements in areas like gas mileage, insulation effectiveness, or home appliance energy efficiency drive down consumers' costs, which then leads to increased use of these goods. It is tough to quantify how much increased use offsets technological improvements, but it is clear that rebound effects occur in automobile use, home energy consumption, and a wide array of other markets (Schor 2010, pp. 87–89).

75. A financial planner whom I was interviewing for another project about socially responsible investment strategies said that a couple of clients had changed their retirement portfolios following the oil spill in the Gulf. One client called him "frantically," saying she "couldn't sleep knowing that my money is going to BP." She pulled all her 401k investments out of mutual funds that contained investments in oil companies.

76. PEW 2010.

77. Putnam 2000.

78. Zukin 2004; Simon 2011.

79. Hilgartner and Bosk (1988) created a theoretical model to highlight the social forces necessary to popularize a social problem. The *novelty* of shopping for a cause, the attempts to *depoliticize* shopping for a cause, and the *drama* associated with stories that allow consumers to believe they can create change through

shopping all align with variables described by Hilgartner and Bosk that allow social problems to enter public arenas.

80. DeCarlo 2007.

81. Brooks 2000. For full disclosure, I moved to Mount Airy while writing this book. I reluctantly align myself with the conscientious consumers that I describe in this book. For instance, my wife and I now own a Kia Sorento, which we refer to as a cross-over utility vehicle (CUV) instead of a sport utility vehicle (SUV). The difference, as far as I can tell, is that a CUV gets the same miles per gallon as an SUV, but it does not come with the same social stigma. We justify this purchase by saying that we "needed" it to transport our two kids.

82. For example, a recent Harris Poll (2008) indicated that 63 percent of American adults "indicated that they would pay more for organic, fair trade, or locally sourced food." The average respondent said he or she would pay between 17 and 19 percent more for these products. Kimeldorf et al. (2006) cite a number of other surveys that also show consumers will pay more for ethically sourced products. Their study is unique because it provide some evidence suggesting that these surveys accurately depict the actions of shoppers. Their findings, although preliminary, suggest that shoppers will act on the pro-social attitudes displayed in these surveys.

83. In *The Social Meaning of Money* (1997), Viviana Zelizer utilizes this approach to explain how consumers earmark money for different purchases. By doing so, they can justify the construction of often-contradictory values inherent in their purchases.

CHAPTER 2

1. Many children do pick coffee on farms selling fair-trade-certified coffee. In Nicaragua, for example, children often do not attend school when coffee is being harvested.

2. The article featuring Joe in *USA Today* was written by Julie Appleby (2007).

3. Roscigno and Danaher 2001.

4. Howard Schultz, chairman and CEO of Starbucks, decided to rapidly open more coffee shops only after visiting Italy in 1983. The trip verified his belief that a chain of Italian-inspired coffee houses would be successful in the United States (Simon 2009, p. 32).

5. In 2000, Robert Putnam published *Bowling Alone*, in which he showed that the rate of Americans' participation in a wide range of collective organizations was falling to historic lows. The title plays off this idea. Putnam explained that more Americans are bowling now than ever, but they no longer bowl in leagues. Fewer Americans are signing petitions, are familiar with their neighbors, or are members of civic organizations than in the past. McPherson et al. (2006, p. 353) also show that the "number of people saying they had no one with whom they discuss important matters nearly tripled" between 1985 and 2004. In a different strand of literature, Oldenberg (1989) describes the importance of third places,

where individuals can meet outside their homes (first places) and workplaces (second places). Third places, such as coffee shops, are important for generating a sense of community and civic engagement.

6. Only six of the fourteen Mexicans found dead were farmers, but most were indirectly dependent on the coffee trade for their income. At the time of the attempted border crossing, the price of coffee was hovering around sixty cents a pound, so it was costing more to grow coffee than it was worth on the open market. Further, the going rate for an illegal border crossing at this time was around $2,000. Farmers tended to use their land to guarantee the loans that were required to make these crossings. Relatives of the immigrants told reporters in 2001 that they feared their land would be taken to repay the loans (Tuckman 2001).

7. Rice 2012.

8. I do not mean to suggest that Judy Wicks is an ethical entrepreneur who is free from criticism. There was much scrutiny of Wicks's purported attempts to deny her staff the right to unionize (Taussig 2006). And there was some debate over the mission-statement clause during the sale of the White Dog. Some disgruntled long-term employees were laid off after the sale of the restaurant and publicly criticized Wicks on a number of prominent websites and blogs in Philadelphia. The swift attack on Wicks underscore the point that moral reputations or "moral power" can be tough to earn and easily challenged (Mehta and Winship 2010).

9. Gould 1993.

10. Joe wants to stress that he also distributed "hundreds" of voter registration cards during this time period. He wanted his customers to be politically engaged, no matter whom they supported. Nevertheless, it was clear that Joe was a strong, albeit critical, supporter of the Democrats.

11. Upon reading this section, Joe said to me, "Was I wrong?" He wanted to emphasize that his point was legitimate and not something that I should take lightly.

12. Bureau of Labor Statistics 2011

13. I am currently an assistant professor at Saint Joseph's University. At the time, however, I was not affiliated with SJU. I was not in the job market, and I did not personally know the faculty members in the sociology department.

14. After reading this section, Joe reiterated that all the other cafés were located in residential neighborhoods that made them more likely to attract parents.

15. Roscigno and Danaher 2001.

16. Joe was not particularly happy with my characterization of him here. He told me that he was really upset during this time period, and he felt that he did not need to hide his angst from others. He said, "Sharing my challenges with others may at first come off as a negative, but by opening up, [other] business owners would share their own experiences."

17. I am again making an argument similar to that of Mehta and Winship (2010), who describe the significance of moral power. Moral power is like a form of

cultural or social capital in that it can be exchanged for economic capital. But it is not durable and can quickly become attacked and weakened.

18. In my first interview with Joe, he said, "There's nothing wrong with [making a profit]. I didn't start a business just because I had nothing better to do. . . . I want to make a profit. I want to be comfortable. I want to be able to retire someday."

CHAPTER 3

1. Kahneman 2011; Collins 2004; Arnould and Price 1993.

2. Kahneman, p. 138.

3. Frederick Wherry (2008) shows how emotional energy shapes the terms of negotiations between buyers and sellers of handicrafts. I discuss the relevance of this "interaction ritual chain" framework, for understanding how promoters become part of the fair trade movement in more depth elsewhere (Brown 2011). See also Goffman (1967).

4. Arnould and Price 1993.

5. Gould's (1993) model for predicting social movement participation states that individuals must believe that their actions are efficiently being directed at the intended social problem. The goal of these trips is to facilitate these beliefs.

6. Upper-level managers at Ten Thousand Villages initially told me that the total retail sales of stores with managers who traveled overseas increased upon the managers' return from these trips. I asked to see data confirming this trend, and they reframed their position, saying that the products that the managers saw being produced are sold at a "higher rate" after the trips than before the trips.

7. At the time of Cindy's presentation, her description of fair trade was pretty accurate. In September 2011, Fair Trade USA ended its relationship with FLO. It no longer requires that farmers be members of cooperatives. "Large farms," alternatively called "plantations," can now receive fair-trade certification from Fair Trade USA.

8. "Special Report: Voting with Your Trolley—Food Politics," *Economist* 381 (8507) (December 9, 2006): 81.

9. During my two brief trips to Nicaragua, I heard fair-trade leaders encouraging farmers to diversify their crops to protect them from the price swings associated with coffee sales. More important, Sarah Lyon (2011) spent a number of years interviewing fair-trade farmers in Guatemala. She saw families encouraging their children to become educated so that they would not be reliant on coffee sales. She also saw families investing their fair-trade surpluses in businesses outside the coffee market. All of these observations provide evidence that fair-trade farmers are aware of the volatile nature of coffee prices and that their commitment to fair trade is not blinding them to the oversupply problem in coffee markets.

10. Much research involves the social processes involved in transforming meanings of commodities. Wherry (2006) describes the transformations in meanings between sacred and profane that occur through the rituals involved in the

production process of the object. Becker (1982) notes the sharp division between crafts and arts. Although they require the same skill sets to produce, crafts and artworks are valued very differently because of the art world and the social interactions surrounding the object. Bourdieu (1984) refers to the tension between art produced for a wide audience and art produced for other artists as a characteristic inherent in a wide range of markets.

11. The search for authenticity motivates many consumers (but not necessarily producers) to participate in this market. Consumers want to know how ethically produced the coffee is and whether or not traditional artisanal techniques were used to produce a handicraft. Finding an object that consumers perceive to be authentic allows them to distinguish themselves from consumers buying mass-produced items. For a discussion of the importance of authenticity on a wide range of markets, see Grazian 2003; Fine 2003; Johnston and Baumann 2010; Peterson 1997; Wherry 2006.

12. These objects were invested with symbolic meaning through my social interactions with the artisans at the Ten Thousand Villages workshop. I had barely noticed these objects in the past, but suddenly they stuck out among the other products in the store (Durkheim [1915] 1995; Collins 2004).

13. Randall Collins's (2004) theory of "interaction ritual chains" suggests that I was filled with emotional energy from my interaction with Illies. That energy spilled into my interaction with this customer but became depleted as the customer did not seem interested in my story. This is similar to what Joe experienced upon returning home from Nicaragua (chapter 2), when he eagerly looked to tell stories about the living conditions of farmers but was faced with customers who could not understand what he had witnessed.

14. Arlie Hochschild (1983) makes the distinction between surface and deep acting among employees. She discusses the commoditization of emotions within the service economy. Surface acting is a type of emotion work that involves consciously putting on an act to convey a certain persona to others. A forced smile is one example. Deep acting is perceived to be more genuine. It involves a real emotional connection deriving from a situation. The "buy more" philosophy fits this perspective.

15. Arnould et al. 2009.

16. Lyon 2011; Lyon and Moberg 2010; Bacon 2005; Littrell and Dickson 1999; Raynolds 2002; Raynolds et al. 2007.

17. The literature describing fair trade's benefits for producer communities is vast and growing rapidly, but few studies specifically compare fair-trade and nonfair-trade communities. Arnould et al. (2009) show that fair-trade premiums provide measurable economic, health, and educational benefits to families growing fair-trade coffee. Jaffee (2007, pp. 131–132) devotes a chapter of *Brewing Justice* to a comparison of nearby fair-trade and nonfair-trade communities. He explains that fair-trade families are, "on average . . . less indebted, their children receive more education, and their homes contain a few additional comforts." Fair-trade

families appear to be doing only marginally better. This difference appears to be a result, in part, of fair-trade families' decision to redistribute their fair-trade premiums by hiring local wage laborers. This "ripple effect" retains a bit more money within the community. Catholic Relief Services is sponsoring a study to compare fair-trade and nonfair-trade coffee communities.

18. Muniz and O'Guinn 2001.

19. Brown 2011.

CHAPTER 4

1. This is consistent with theories that describe consumer identities as fleeting, fragmented, and fluid (McCracken 1986; Bauman 2000). This finding also points to the contradiction inherent in the notion of a citizen-consumer within a profit-oriented market (Johnston 2008). A growing number of sociologists, anthropologists, and marketers are focusing on the contexts and social forces (rather than only on values or attitudes) that influence shopping patterns. See Arnould and Thompson (2005) for a comprehensive review of this literature.

2. Kimeldorf et al. 2006; Matathia and Salzman 1999 ; see Kimeldorf et al. (2006) for a discussion of the survey confirming that a majority of consumers are willing to pay a premium for products designated as having been produced under good working conditions. Matathia and Saltzman (1999) explain that marketers need to be prepared for an influx of consumers who care about where products come from, who made them, and how the environment is impacted by production.

3. David Halle (1993) makes a similar claim when talking about American's preference for abstract art. Many respondents spoke of their appreciation of this art in their home by stressing that it matched the sofa. They pointed to the aesthetics of the art, rather than stressing their deep love for the style of a particular artist. Josee Johnston and Shyon Baumann (2010) make a similar claim when they show that ethical discourse among "foodies" is subsumed by an emphasis on taste and quality. Johnston and her colleagues (2011) also found that consumers with a conscience are reluctant to draw sharp moral boundaries between themselves and others. Instead, they choose to distinguish themselves from others by focusing on the quality and health-promoting characteristics of the food they eat.

4. Goffman 1959.

5. Tim Clydesdale explains that first-year college students act in a similar manner by keeping their identities in a "lockbox." They avoid conflict with their peers by avoiding controversial ethical and political discussions. Nina Eliasoph (1998) shows that Americans avoid potentially polarizing, front-stage political discourse but will talk about these issues in more restricted backstage settings.

6. Kaufman 2008; National Renewable Energy Laboratory 2011.

7. Prasad et al. 2004.

8. Conroy 2007.

9. "Scientists Work to Develop Environmentally Friendly Bombs" 2008.
10. Slater (2010) writes, "the critical study of consumption—as opposed to the instrumentalist orientation of marketing and business studies—barely existed except as a patrician dismissal of everyday life in the modern world. Whether in the name of elitist disdain or anti-capitalist politics—or scary marriages of the two—this entire space in which people make up and reproduce life, mediated by material and symbolic things, was treated as a mere index or symptom of the pathologies of the social structures that ostensibly 'explained' consumption. This was intellectually and politically disabling as well as ethically disrespectful" (p. 280).
11. Canclini 2001.
12. Simon (2011) introduced the concept of the "rough democracy of buying" while Micheletti and Follesdal (2007) discuss the "push" and "pull" of markets.
13. Mazar and Zhong 2010.
14. Zelizer 1997.
15. Monin and Miller 2001; Sachdeva et al. 2009.
16. Mazar and Zhong 2010.
17. Schwartz 2004.
18. Karl's trajectory of consumer activism seems to fit the profile described by Janet Lorenzen (2012) in her article "Going Green: The Process of Lifestyle Change." Lorenzen writes that green lifestyles are experienced as both "a work in progress and a provisionally coherent life narrative."
19. Blau 1964; Mauss 1997; Miller 1998; McCracken 1986; Ruth et al. 1999; Sherry 1983.
20. I discuss the social dynamics that govern how and when consumers talk about social responsibility in more depth elsewhere (Brown 2009).
21. Boltanski and Thevenot 2006.
22. Marketers spend a good amount of time analyzing the factors beyond food that influence how we think about taste. Brian Wansink explains in *Mindless Eating* (2006) that we make more than two hundred choices a day about food. We often think little about how factors such as plate or cup size influence how much we eat or drink. I am arguing here that fair-trade certification influences how we think about product quality and taste. For some, it's a positive; for others, it is not.
23. Interestingly, Keri's decision to critique aesthetics and quality echoes a (presumably unintended) strategy of consumer culture critics of the mid-twentieth century. Members of the Frankfurt School extended Karl Marx's conflict theory into the realm of consumption right at the time when consumers and retailers were beginning to gain more power over conventional supply chains (Cohen 2003; Shell 2009). Members of the Frankfurt School believed that consumers were duped into buying products they did not need. Consumers were exploited by the profit-driven culture industries in much the same ways that the proletariat was exploited by the bourgeoisie. Instead, of emphasizing morality as Juliet Schor

(2010, p. 275) explains, the Frankfurt School's "complaints were on aesthetic grounds, (ugliness or banality of consumer culture), its political characteristics (conformist, authoritarian, manipulative), practical effects such as its impact on the environment, and its 'self-defeating' nature (in the case of 'treadmill' models of relative consumption)."

24. Cracker Barrel executives issued a memo saying that the company did not want to hire people who did not demonstrate "normal heterosexual values." In 2003, the company changed its nondiscrimination policy to include sexual orientation. Nevertheless, by 2010, the company was still voted the third worst place to work for gays in the United States by the Human Rights Campaign (Huffington Post 2010).

25. As the sociologist Robert Wuthnow (1996) explains, consumer decisions are often more ritualistic and emotive than rational and calculating. To back up his point, Wuthnow describes a wealthy man living in a luxurious house who incessantly turns off the lights in his home to save money. The man can afford to keep the lights on, but, by turning them off, he reinforces his identity as someone who was taught to avoid waste.

26. Matathia and Salzman 1999; Kimeldorf et al. 2006; Krier 2008.

27. Ehrich and Irwin 2005.

28. The literature on symbolic and social boundaries surrounding moral issues is vast. Pierre Bourdieu argues that moral boundaries are deployed only by individuals who are upwardly or downwardly mobile (1984). Michelle Lamont, by contrast, argues that both working and upper-middle class men in the United States and in France make moral (as well as cultural and economic) distinctions among themselves and others (1992, 2000). Her work reinvigorated the study of symbolic boundaries (see Lamont and Molnar 2002), but some observers have claimed that moral boundaries are more permeable and fleeting than her model implies (Brown 2009; Sherman 2005).

CHAPTER 5

1. Lazor 2007.

2. As I finish writing this book, Carmichael finalized a new line of coffees endorsed by Leonardo DiCaprio. The goal is to model the coffee on Paul Newman's line of products and to donate 100 percent of the profits to various charities. My goal is not to criticize Carmichael but to show how entrepreneurs fight for conscientious consumers' attention. Michaele Weissman's book *God in a Cup* does an excellent job profiling third-wave coffee entrepreneurs who have company policies similar to Carmichael's. She chronicles the tensions they face as they try to find social benefits for individual farmers and farming communities while still searching for the highest-quality beans.

3. Randall Collins (1998) refers to this as a "limited attention space." Individuals or, in this case, organizations compete to capture the attention of the media and consumers.

4. Bourdieu 1993.

5. For Bourdieu (1984, 1993), the field of cultural production is largely structured by economic and cultural capital. In most instances, Bourdieu argues, moral capital does not play a significant role in organizing the production of cultural goods. Lamont, however, has shown that moral boundaries are a way in which French and American men distinguish themselves from others (Lamont 1992, 2000). The ethical turn in markets offers a new context in which to study the extent to which morals provide a marker of social distinction. We can clearly see organizations competing for altruism within these markets. Admittedly, there is evidence that individuals are still reluctant to enact strong moral boundaries in everyday life (chapter 4; see also Sherman 2005).

6. Pinker 2008.

7. See Eliasoph (1998) for an interesting parallel with the ways Americans talk about politics.

8. Kopytoff 1986.

9. Ehrich and Irwin (2005) show that even consumers who care deeply about certain issues, such as not buying wood that was harvested from a rainforest, will avoid asking questions about the product if they feel the answers will conflict with their value system.

10. Micheletti and Follesdal 2007.

11. Cohen 2003; Glickman 2009.

12. Glickman 2009. To give just one example, more than 5,000 products with fair-trade certification were sold in 2004 (Nicholls and Opal 2004), and today there are more than 10,000 products with fair-trade certification (Fair Trade USA 2012).

13. Klein 2001.

14. Leidner 1993; Ritzer 2011.

15. Shell 2009.

16. Lyderson 2006.

17. Shell 2009, pp. 127–128.

18. Tucker 1972, p. 667.

19. Brooks 2000.

20. Schor 1998; Simon 2009.

21. Simon 2009.

22. See chapter 2 for more about this issue.

23. Simon 2009. This is the best estimate that I have come across. It is based on research for Bryant Simon's book, *Everything but the Coffee* (2009).

24. This issue came up quite often at the 2005 Fair Trade Futures conference in Chicago. Many of the attendees flew into the conference and noticed a Starbucks advertisement in the free airline magazine. The ad included a prominent Fair Trade USA logo showing that Starbucks sold fair-trade coffee. The advertisement implied that all of Starbucks' coffee was fair-trade-certified. This infuriated the attendees who were committed to selling only fair-trade coffee. Many attendees

were upset with Starbucks and Fair Trade USA for allowing this misleading advertisement.

25. Klein 2001.
26. The article cited in the Civic Association meeting is here: Nelson (2005). One of the keys to Philadelphia's future, according to Nelson, is attracting the people to whom Richard Florida (2002) refers as the "creative class."
27. Cole 2008.
28. Gary Alan Fine (2004) explains how self-taught artists are greatly valued for their position outside the traditional art world. They are viewed as more pure, more authentic, and more natural and as artists who are not looking to make a profit. His findings apply here, as it is the stories behind the artisans that greatly influence the perceived value of the product itself. Behavioral economists are also beginning to incorporate identity into their economic models as a variable that influences market activity (Akerloff and Kranton 2010). The emphasis on both stories and the ethnic heritage of the producers runs the risk of exoticizing producers (Said 1994; Cole 2008).
29. Forero 2001.
30. Forero 2004.
31. Moberg and Lyon 2010, p. 8.
32. See Johnston and Baumann 2007.
33. Cole 2008.
34. Cohen 2010.
35. "Credit Card Debt Statistics" 2011.
36. Schor 2010, p. 9.
37. Samantha King's *Pink Ribbon, Inc.* (2006) takes a critical look at how the Susan G. Komen Foundation spends its pink-ribbon money. All of the money goes toward finding a cure for breast cancer, whereas none of the money goes toward reducing environmental causes of breast cancer. A few products, with known carcinogens in them are still able to put the pink ribbon on their packaging. But if your goal is to gain status among ethical consumers, you might not want to talk about these issues. You might come off as "too preachy!"

CHAPTER 6

1. Fisher 2006.
2. Rothschild-Whitt 1979.
3. Ten Thousand Villages 2010.
4. Fair Trade Institute 2012. The Fair Trade Institute provides a dynamic database of current papers and books that examine how fair trade impacts producers. This book was particularly informed by a wide range of scholarship on this issue, including Moberg and Lyon 2010; Lyon 2011; DeCarlo 2007; Jaffee 2007; Raynolds et al. 2007; Bacon 2005; Grimes and Milgram 2000; Littrell and Dickson 1999; Nicholls and Opal 2004; Raynolds 2002; Simpson and Rapone 2000; Tarmann 2002; Leclair 2003; and Levi and Linton 2003.

5. Lyon and Moberg 2010; Lyon 2011; Jaffee 2007.

6. Lyon and Moberg 2010.

7. Lyon 2010.

8. Lyon 2011. While traveling throughout Nicaragua, I learned of similar attempts to diversify farmers' crops so that they would not be so vulnerable to changes in coffee prices.

9. Forero 2004.

10. Moberg and Lyon 2010, p. 17.

11. Jaffee 2007; Arnould et al. 2009; Lyon 2011; Raynolds 2002; Raynolds et al. 2007.

12. Jacqueline is the senior program adviser for the Economic Justice and Fair Trade programs at CRS. Shayna is now the cocoa sustainability manager for Mars Global Chocolate. Erin is currently the CEO of Divine USA.

13. See Dean Cycon's book *Java Trekker: Dispatches from the World of Fair Trade Coffee* (2007) for an example of a great mission-driven storyteller.

14. Nicholls and Opal 2004; Jaffee 2007.

15. Said 1994.

16. Doane 2010.

17. Eliasoph 1998.

18. Brown 2009.

19. Clydesdale 2007.

20. Ansolabehere and Iyengar 1995.

21. Perrin 2006, p. 43.

22. Lamont 1992, 2000.

23. See Miller 2001.

24. Raynolds et al. 2007.

25. I am referring to different ways of thinking about power as outlined by Steven Lukes (2005). Fair traders are looking to revise the acceptable forms of trade (reform), rather than change the whole system of trade by overthrowing capitalism (radical).

26. Moberg and Lyon 2010, p. 7.

27. Simon 2009.

28. Tucker 1972.

29. Micheletti and Follesdal 2007, p. 174.

30. Shell 2009, p. 29.

31. Schor 2010.

32. A special issue of *Psychology and Marketing* edited by Stephen Zavestoski also addresses this issue by exploring the rationale for consumers' anticonsumption attitudes. Researchers suggest that even consumers who are critical of overconsumption may be more willing to shop for a cause if marketers pay closer attention to their needs. Adbusters readers may be attracted to products that are marketed as being critical of consumer culture (Rumbo 2002); ethical consumers search for authentic goods that align with their ideals (Shaw and Newholm 2002); voluntary simplifiers may be searching for goods that can allow them to

feel more authentic (Zavestoski 2002) and for products that emphasize function-ality over status (Craig-Lees and Hill 2002); and marketers can reduce African American adolescent girls' resistance to the ideals of beauty portrayed in the mainstream media by increasing realistic portrayals that match their concep-tions of femininity (Duke 2002). All of this research indicates that a deeper probing of the desires of those who resist consumption could lead to a reorgani-zation of markets.

33. Schor and Willis 2009.
34. Williams 2007.
35. TransFair USA 2010.
36. Szasz 2007.
37. Miller 2001, p. 226.
38. Miller 2001, p. 234.

APPENDIX

1. Bourdieu 1993, 2003.

BIBLIOGRAPHY

Akerloff, George, and Rachel Kranton. 2010. *Identity Economics: How Our Identities Shape Our Work, Wages, and Well-Being*. Princeton, NJ: Princeton University Press.

Ansolabehere, Stephen, and Shanto Iyengar. 1995. *Going Negative: How Attack Ads Shrink and Polarize the Electorate*. New York: Free Press.

Appleby, Julie. 2007. "Who's Uninsured in 2007? Its More than Just the Poor." *USA Today*. March 14.

Arnould, Eric, and Craig Thompson. 2005. "Consumer Culture Theory (CCT): Twenty Years of Research." *Journal of Consumer Research* 31: 868–883.

Arnould, Eric, Alejandro Plastina, and Dwayne Ball. 2009. "Does Fair Trade Deliver on Its Core Value Proposition? Effects on Income, Educational Attainment, and Health in Three Countries." *Journal of Public Policy and Marketing* 28 (Fall): 2l.

Arnould, Eric, and Linda Price. 1993. "River Magic: Extraordinary Experience and the Extended Service Encounter." *Journal of Consumer Research* 20: 24–45.

Bacon, Christopher. 2005. "Confronting the Coffee Crisis: Can Fair Trade, Organic, and Specialty Coffees Reduce Small-Scale Farmer Vulnerability in Northern Nicaragua." *World Development* 33: 497–511.

Bauman, Zygmunt. 2000. *Liquid Modernity*. Cambridge, UK: Polity.

Becker, Howard. 1982. *Art Worlds*. Berkeley: University of California Press.

Binkley, Sam. 2003. "The Seers of Menlo Park: The Discourse of Heroic Consumption in the 'Whole Earth Catalog." *Journal of Consumer Culture* 3(3): 283–313.

Blau, Pierre. 1964. *Exchange and Power in Social Life*. New York: Wiley.

Boltanski, Luc, and Laurent Thevenot. 2006. *On Justification: Economies of Worth*. Princeton, NJ: Princeton University Press.

Bourdieu, Pierre. 1984. *Distinction*. Cambridge, MA: Harvard University Press.

Bourdieu, Pierre. 1990. *The Logic of Practice*. Stanford, CA: Stanford University Press.

Bourdieu, Pierre. 1993. *The Field of Cultural Production*. New York: Columbia University Press.

Bourdieu, Pierre. 2003. *Outline of a Theory of Practice*. New York: Cambridge University Press.

Brooks, David. 2000. *Bobos in Paradise*. New York: Touchstone.

Brown, Keith. 2008. "Framing a Fair Trade Life: Tensions in the Fair Trade Marketplace." In *Lived Experiences of Public Consumption*, ed. Daniel Thomas Cook. New York: Palgrave Macmillan.

Brown, Keith. 2009. "The Social Dynamics and Durability of Moral Boundaries." *Sociological Forum* 24: 4.

Brown, Keith. 2011. "Interaction Ritual Chains and the Mobilization of Conscientious Consumers." *Qualitative Sociology* 34: 121–141.

Bureau of Labor Statistics. 2011. "Employment Status of the Population, 1940s–Present." http://www.bls.gov/cps/cpsaatl.pdf, accessed June 15, 2011.

CAN. 2011. "CAN Official Statement." *CAN Alliance of Fair Trade Producer Network's Response to Fair Trade USA's Decision to Drop FLO Certification.* http://clac-comerciojusto.org/media/descargas/can-official-statement-20110928-pdf-2011-09-29-11-10-27.pdf, accessed January 19, 2012.

Canclini, Nestor Garcia. 2001. *Consumers and Citizens: Globalization and Multicultural Conflicts.* Minneapolis: University of Minnesota Press.

Clydesdale, Tim. 2007. *The First Year Out: Understanding American Teens after High School.* Chicago: University of Chicago Press.

Cohen, Lizabeth. 2003. *A Consumer's Republic: The Politics of Mass Consumption in Postwar America.* New York: Vintage Books.

Cohen, Maurie. 2010. "The International Political Economy of (Un)sustainable Consumption and the Global Financial Collapse." *Environmental Politics* 19(1): 107–126.

Cole, Nicki L. 2008. "Global Capitalism Organizing Knowledge of Race, Gender and Class: The Case of Socially Responsible Coffee." *Race, Gender, and Class* 15(1/2): 170–187.

Collins, Randall. 1998. *The Sociology of Philosophies: A Global Theory of Intellectual Change.* Cambridge, MA: Harvard University Press.

Collins, Randall. 2004. *Interaction Ritual Chains.* Princeton, NJ: Princeton University Press.

Conroy, Michael. 2007. *Branded! How the "Certification Revolution" Is Transforming Global Corporations.* Canada: New Society.

Craig-Lees, Margaret, and Constance Hill. 2002. "Understanding Voluntary Simplifiers." *Psychology and Marketing* 19(2): 187–210.

"Credit Card Debt Statistics." 2011. *Money-Zine.com.* http://www.money-zine.com/Financial-Planning/Debt-Consolidation/Credit-Card-Debt-Statistics/, accessed December 12, 2011.

Cycon, Dean. 2007. *Java Trekker: Dispatches from the World of Fair Trade Coffee.* White River Junction, VT: Chelsea Green.

DeCarlo, Jacqueline. 2007. *Fair Trade: Beginner's Guide.* Oxford: Oneworld Publications.

Doane, Molly. 2010. "Relationship Coffees: Structure and Agency in the Fair Trade System." In *Fair Trade and Social Justice,* ed. S. Lyon and M. Moberg. New York: New York University Press.

Duke, Lisa. 2002. "Get Real!: Cultural Relevance and Resistance to the Mediated Feminine Ideal." *Psychology and Marketing* 19(2): 211–233.

Durkheim, Emile. [1915] 1995. *The Elementary Forms of Religious Life.* New York: Free Press.

Ehrenreich, Barbara. 2001. *Nickle and Dimed: On (Not) Getting by in America.* New York: Metropolitan Books.

Ehrich, Kristine, and Julie Irwin. 2005. "Willful Ignorance in the Request of Product Attribute Information." *Journal of Marketing Research* 52: 266–277.

Eliasoph, Nina. 1998. *Avoiding Politics: How Americans Produce Apathy in Everyday Life*. New York: Cambridge University Press.

Equal Exchange. 2011. "Our Co-op. Our Story." http://www.equal exchange.coop/story, accessed June 13, 2011.

Fair Trade Institute. 2012. Fair Trade Database of Academic Publications. Produced in partnership with the Fair Trade Resource Network. http://www.fairtrade-institute .org/, accessed February 2, 2012.

Fairtrade Labeling Organizations Association. 2011. "An Open Letter from CEO on Changes to the Fairtrade System." Press release, September 16. http://www.fairtrade .net/single_view1.html?&cHash=899072e6c8f75ef575b58a4070427151&tx_ttnews[tt_ news]=237, accessed August 9, 2012.

Fair Trade Research Network (FTRN). 2011. "A Community Discussion of TransFair's Name Change to Fair Trade USA, and Pending Service Mark Application." Webinar 105, February 2. https://docs.google.com/leaf?id=0B43dCZ7zYP61OWRhNjhjMTgt ZmNiMyooNjdhLWFhN2UtMDkzNjQoNzNkNzll&hl=en&authkey =CO2DjZkE, accessed January 18, 2012.

Fair Trade USA. 2010. "TransFair USA Changes Name to Fair Trade USA." Press release, September 16. http://fairtradeusa.org/press-room/press_release/transfair -usa-changes-name-fair-trade-usa, accessed January 18, 2012.

Fair Trade USA. 2011a. "Fair Trade USA Financial Statements: December 31 2010 and 2009." Armanino McKenna (CPA). July 20. http://www.fairtradeusa.org/sites/ default/files/2010%20Audited%20Financial%20Statements.pdf, accessed February 8, 2012.

Fair Trade USA. 2011b. "Fair Trade USA 2010 Almanac." http://www.fairtradeusa.org/ sites/default/files/Almanac%202010_0.pdf, accessed October 31, 2011.

Fair Trade USA. 2012. "Fair Trade Just a Click Away with New 'Fair Trade Finder' App." Fair Trade USA. http://fairtradeusa.org/blog/fair-trade-just-click-away-new-fair -trade-finder-app, accessed February 14, 2012.

Fine, Gary Alan. 2003. "Crafting Authenticity: The Validation of Identity in Self-Taught Art." *Theory and Society* 32: 253–180.

Fine, Gary Alan. 2004. *Everyday Genius: Self-Taught Art and the Culture of Authenticity*. Chicago: University of Chicago Press.

Fisher, Dana. 2006. *Activism, Inc*. Stanford, CA: Stanford University Press.

Florida, Richard. 2002. *The Rise of the Creative Class: And How It's Transforming Work, Leisure, Community, and Everyday Life*. New York: Basic Books.

Forero, Juan. 2001. "A Coffee Icon Rides His Mule Off into the Sunset." *New York Times*, November 24.

Forero, Juan. 2004. "Colombians Urged to Drink More and Better Coffee (Their Own)." *New York Times*, May 29.

Giddens, Anthony. 2000. *Runaway World: How Globalization Is Reshaping Our Lives*. New York: Routledge.

Gladwell, Malcolm. 2000. *The Tipping Point: How Little Things Can Make a Big Difference*. New York: Little, Brown.

Glickman, Lawrence. 2009. *Buying Power: A History of Consumer Activism in America*. Chicago: University of Chicago Press.

Global Exchange. 2012. Description on Global Exchange Homepage. http://www.globalexchange.org/, accessed February 8, 2012.

Goffman, Erving. 1959. *The Presentation of Self in Everyday Life*. New York: Anchor.

Goffman, Erving. 1967. *Interaction Ritual*. New York: Pantheon Books.

Goodman, Michael. 2004. "Reading Fair Trade: Political Ecological Imaginary and the Moral Economy of Fair Trade Foods." *Political Geography* 23: 891–915.

Gould, Roger. 1993. "Collective Action and Network Structure." *American Sociological Review* 58: 182–196.

Grazian, David. 2003. *Blue Chicago: The Search for Authenticity in Urban Blues Clubs*. Chicago: University of Chicago Press.

Grimes, Kimberly M., and B. Lynne Milgram, eds. 2000. *Artisans and Cooperatives: Developing Alternative Trade for the Global Economy*. Tucson: University of Arizona Press.

Griskevicius, Vladas, Joshua Tybur, and Bran Van den Bergh. 2010. "Going Green to Be Seen: Status, Reputation, and Conspicuous Conservation." *Journal of Personality and Social Psychology* 98(3): 392–404.

Halle, David. 1993. *Inside Culture: Art and Class in the American Home*. Chicago: University of Chicago Press.

Harris Poll. 2008. "SCA Survey Conducted by Harris Interactive Shows That Despite a Weakened Economy, U.S. Consumers Willing to Spend Green to Go Green." Harris Interactive, April 21. http://www.harrisinteractive.com/vault/Client_ News_ SCA_2008_04.pdf, accessed February 10, 2012.

Hilgartner, Stephen, and Charles L. Bosk. 1988. "The Rise and Fall of Social Problems: A Public Arenas Model." *American Journal of Sociology* 94(1): 53–78.

Hochschild, Arlie R. 1983. *The Managed Heart: Commercialization of Human Feeling*. Berkeley: University of California Press.

Holt, Douglas. 2000. "Does Cultural Capital Structure American Consumption?" In *The Consumer Society Reader*, ed. Juliet Schor and Douglas Holt. New York: New Press.

Huffington Post. 2010. "The Worst Companies for LGBT Workers: HRC's 2010 Ranking." Huffington Post Business, April 11. http://www.huffingtonpost.com/2010/02/09/the-least-lgbt-worst-plac_n_454745.html, accessed January 11, 2012.

International Coffee Organization (ICO). 2012. "Historical Data: ICO Indicator Prices in U.S. Cents per Pound." http://www.ico.org/historical/2000+/PDF/HIST-PRICES.pdf, accessed January 10, 2012.

International Trade Administration. 1998. "International Visitors (Inbound) and U.S. Residents (Outbound) (1988–1997)." http://tinet.ita.doc.gov/view/f-1997-06-001/index.html, accessed February 8, 2012.

International Trade Administration. 2010. "U.S. Citizen Air Traffic to Overseas

Regions, Canada and Mexico 2010." http://tinet.ita.doc.gov/view/m-2010-O-001/index.html, accessed February 8, 2012.

Jaffee, Daniel. 2007. *Brewing Justice: Fair Trade Coffee, Sustainability, and Survival.* Berkeley: University of California Press.

Johnston, Josee. 2008. "The Citizen-Consumer Hybrid: Ideological Tensions and the Case of Whole Foods Market." *Theory and Society* 37: 229–270.

Johnston, Josee, and Shyon Baumann. 2007. "Democracy versus Distinction: A Study of Omnivorousness in Gourmet Food Writing." *American Journal of Sociology* 113(1): 165–204.

Johnston, Josee, and Shyon Baumann. 2010. *Foodies: Democracy and Distinction in the Gourmet Foodscape.* New York: Routledge.

Johnston, Josee, Michelle Szabo, and Alexandra Rodney. 2011. "Good Food, Good People: Understanding the Cultural Repertoire of Ethical Eating." *Journal of Consumer Culture* 11(3): 293–318.

Kahneman, Daniel. 2011. *Thinking, Fast and Slow.* New York: Farrar, Straus and Giroux.

Kaufman, Joanne. 2008. "Completely Unplugged, Fully Green." *New York Times,* October 19. http://www.nytimes.com/2008/10/19/style/19iht-19greenorexia.17083793.html?scp=1&sq=Completely%20Unplugged%20Fully%20Green&st=cse, accessed January 30, 2012.

Kimeldorf, Howard, Rachel Meyer, Monica Prasad, and Ian Robinson. 2006. "Consumers with a Conscience: Will They Pay More?" *Contexts* 5(1): 24–29.

King, Samantha. 2006. *Pink Ribbon, Inc.* Minneapolis: University of Minnesota Press.

Klein, Naomi. 2001. *No Logo.* London: Flamingo.

Kopytoff, Igor. 1986. "The Cultural Biography of Things: Commoditization as Process." In *The Social Life of Things: Commodities in Cultural Perspective*, ed. A. Appadurai. Cambridge: Cambridge University Press.

Krier, Jean-Marie. 2008. "Fair Trade 2007: Facts and Figures from an Ongoing Success Story." http://www.fairhelp.nl/home/files/ff_2007.pdf, accessed January 30, 2012.

Lamont, Michele. 1992. *Money, Morals, and Manners: The Culture of the French and American Upper-Middle Class.* Chicago: University of Chicago Press.

Lamont, Michele. 2000. *The Dignity of Working Men: Morality and the Boundaries of Race, Class, and Immigration.* Cambridge, MA: Harvard University Press.

Lamont, Michele, and Virag Molnar. 2002. "The Study of Boundaries in the Social Sciences." *Annual Review of Sociology* 28: 167–195.

Lazor, Drew. 2007. "Caffeine Rush." *City Paper* (Philadelphia), November 20.

Leclair, Mark. 2003. "Fighting Back: The Growth of Alternative Trade." *Development* 46(1): 66–73.

Leidner, Robin. 1993. *Fast Food, Fast Talk: Service Work and the Routinization of Everyday Life.* Berkeley: University of California Press.

Levi, Margaret, and April Linton. 2003. "Fair Trade: A Cup at a Time?" *Politics and Society* 31(3): 407–432.

Littrell, Mary Ann, and Marsha Dickson 1999. *Social Responsibility in the Global Market: Fair Trade of Cultural Products.* Thousand Oaks, CA: Sage.

Livestrong. 2012. "Our History." http://www.livestrong.org/Who-We-Are/Our-History/ Milestones, accessed January 12, 2012.

Lorenzen, Janet. 2012. "Going Green: The Process of Lifestyle Change." *Sociological Forum* 27(1): 94–116.

Lukes, Steven. 2005. *Power: A Radical View*, 2nd ed. New York: Palgrave MacMillan.

Lyderson, Kari. 2006. "Target: Wal-Mart Lite." *CorpWatch*. April 20. http://www .corpwatch.org/article.php?id=13508, accessed February 1, 2012.

Lyon, Sarah. 2010. "A Market of Our Own: Women's Livelihoods and Fair Trade Markets." In *Fair Trade and Social Justice: Global Ethnographies*, ed. Sarah Lyon and Mark Moberg. New York: New York University Press.

Lyon, Sarah. 2011. *Coffee and Community: Maya Farmers and Fair-Trade Markets*. Boulder: University Press of Colorado.

Lyon, Sarah, and Mark Moberg, eds. 2010. *Fair Trade and Social Justice: Global Ethnographies*. New York: New York University Press.

Marx, Karl. 1978. "Economic and Philosophic Manuscripts of 1844." In *The Marx-Engels Reader*, 2nd ed., ed. Robert Tucker. New York: Norton.

Matathia, Ira, and Marian Salzman. 1999. *Next: Trends for the Near Future*. New York: Overlook.

Mauss, Marcel. 1997. *The Gift: Forms and Functions of Exchange in Archaic Societies*. London: Cohen and West.

Mazar, Nina, and Chen-Bo Zhong. 2010. "Do Green Products Make Us Better People?" *Psychological Science* 21(4): 494–498.

McCracken, Grant. 1986. "Culture and Consumption: A Theoretical Account of the Structure and Movement of the Cultural Meaning of Consumer Goods." *Journal of Consumer Research* 13: 71–84.

McPherson, Miller, Lynn Smith-Lovin, and Matthew Brashears. 2006. "Social Isolation in America: Changes in Core Discussion Networks over Two Decades." *American Sociological Review* 71: 353–375.

Mehta, Jal, and Christopher Winship. 2010. "Moral Power." In *Handbook of the Sociology of Morality*, ed. S. Hitlin and S. Vaisey. New York: Springer Science and Business Media.

Micheletti, Michele, and Andreas Follesdal. 2007. "Shopping for Human Rights. An Introduction to the Special Issue." *Journal of Consumer Policy* 30: 167–175.

Miller, Daniel. 1998. *A Theory of Shopping*. Ithaca, NY: Cornell University Press.

Miller, Daniel. 2001. "The Poverty of Morality." *Journal of Consumer Culture* 1(2): 225–243.

Moberg, Mark, and Sarah Lyon. 2010. "What's Fair: The Paradox of Seeking Justice through Markets." In *Fair Trade and Social Justice: Global Ethnographies*, ed. S. Lyon and M. Moberg. New York: New York University Press.

Monin, Benoît, and Dale T. Miller. 2001. "Moral Credentials and the Expression of Prejudice." *Journal of Personality and Social Psychology* 81: 33–43.

Muniz, Albert, Jr., and Thomas O'Guinn. 2001. "Brand Community." *Journal of Consumer Research* 27: 412–432.

National Renewable Energy Laboratory. 2011. "Consumer Attitudes about Renewable Energy: Trends and Regional Differences." Natural Marketing Institute, Harleysville, PA. http://apps3.eere.energy.gov/greenpower/ pdfs/50988.pdf, accessed February 14, 2012.

Nelson, Andrew. 2005. "Next Great City: Philly, Really." *National Geographic Traveler* 22(7): 48–54, 56.

Nicholls, Alex, and Charlotte Opal. 2004. *Fair Trade: Market-Driven Ethical Consumption*. Thousand Oaks, CA: Sage.

Norris, Floyd. 2008. "It's Easier to Be Green if It Also Saves Money." *New York Times, Business*, May 31.

Oldenburg, Ray. 1989. *The Great Good Place: Cafes, Coffee Shops, Bookstores, Bars, Hair Salons, and Other Hangouts at the Heart of a Community*. New York: Marlowe.

Osorio, Nestor. 2002. "The Global Coffee Crisis: A Threat to Sustainable Development." Submission to the World Summit on Sustainable Development, Johannesburg. http://dev.ico.org/documents/globalcrisise.pdf, accessed June 2011.

Paige, Jeffery M. 1997. *Coffee and Power: Revolution and the Rise of Democracy in Central America*. Cambridge, MA: Harvard University Press.

Pendergrast, Mark. 2010. *Uncommon Grounds: The History of Coffee and How It Transformed Our World*. New York: Basic Books.

Perrin, Andrew. 2005. *Citizen Speak: The Democratic Imagination in American Life*. Chicago: University of Chicago Press.

Peterson, Richard. 1997. *Creating Country Music: Fabricating Authenticity*. Chicago: University of Chicago Press.

PEW Research Center for the People and the Press. 2010. "Public Trust in Government: 1958–2010." April 18. http://www.people-press.org/2010/04/18/public-trust-in-government-1958-2010, accessed January 18, 2012.

Pinker, Steven. 2008. "The Moral Instinct." *New York Times Magazine*. http:// www.nytimes.com/2008/01/13/magazine/13Psychologyt.html ?pagewanted=all, accessed January 18, 2008.

PR Newswire. 2011. "SC Johnson Settles Case Involving Greenlist Labeling" July 8. http://www.prnewswire.com/news-releases/sc-johnson-settles-cases-involving-greenlist-labeling-125222089.html, accessed February 8, 2012.

Prasad, Monica, Howard Kimeldorf, Rachel Meyer, and Ian Robinson. 2004. "Consumers of the World Unite: A Market-Based Response to Sweatshops." *Labor Studies Journal* 29(3): 57–79.

Putnam, Robert. 2000. *Bowling Alone: The Collapse and Revival of American Community*. New York: Simon and Schuster.

Raynolds, Laura. 2002. "Poverty Alleviation through Participation in Fair Trade Coffee Networks: Existing Research and Critical Issues," Community and Resource Development Program, The Ford Foundation. http://are.berkeley.edu/courses/EEP131/fall2007/Fairtrade/Raynolds.pdf , accessed August 9, 2012.

Raynolds, Laura, Douglas Murray, and John Wilkinson, eds. 2007. *Fair Trade: The Challenges of Transforming Globalization*. New York: Routledge.

Rice, Paul. 2012. "Fair Trade USA: Why We Parted Ways with Fair Trade International." *Triple Pundit: People, Planet, Profit.* January 11, 2012. http://www. triplepundit .com/2012/01/fair-trade-all-fair-trade-usa-plans-double-impact-2015/, accessed January 18, 2012.

Richey, Lisa Ann, and Stefano Ponte. 2011. *Brand Aid: Shopping Well to Save the World.* Minneapolis: University of Minnesota Press.

Ritzer, George. 2010. *Enchanting a Disenchanted World.* Thousand Oaks, CA: Pine Forge.

Ritzer, George. 2011. *The McDonaldization of Society.* Thousand Oaks, CA: Pine Forge.

Robinson, Phyllis. 2011. "To Tell the Truth: Who Owns Fair Trade?" *Small Farmers. Big Change.* February 1. http://smallfarmersbigchange.coop/2011/02/01/to-tell-the -truth-who-owns-fair-trade-2/, accessed January 19, 2012.

Rodney, Alexandra, Josee Johnston, and Michelle Szabo. 2011. "Good Food, Good People: Understanding the Cultural Repertoire of Ethical Eating." *Journal of Consumer Culture* 11(3): 293–318.

Roscigno, Vincent, and William Danaher. 2001. "Media and Mobilization: The Case of Radio and Southern Textile Worker Insurgency." *American Sociological Review* 66 (February): 21–48.

Rothschild-Whitt, Joyce. 1979. "The Collectivist Organization: An Alternative to Rational-Bureaucratic Models." *American Sociological Review* 44: 509–527.

Rumbo, Joseph. 2002. "Consumer Resistance in a World of Advertising Clutter: The Case of *Adbusters.*" *Psychology and Marketing* 19(2): 127–148.

Ruth, Julie A., Cele C. Otnes, and Frédéric F. Brunel. 1999. "Gift Receipt and the Reformulation of Interpersonal Relationships." *Journal of Consumer Research* 25: 385–402.

Sachdeva, Sonya, Rumen Iliev, and Douglas L. Medin. 2009. "Sinning Saints and Saintly Sinners: The Paradox of Moral Self-Regulation." *Psychological Science* 20: 523–528.

Said, Edward. 1994. *Orientalism.* New York: Vintage Books.

Schneider, Greg. 2004. "Toyota's Prius Proving to Be the Hotter Ride in Hybrids." *Washington Post Business.* http://www.washingtonpost.com/ac2/wp-dyn/A24832 -2004Aug22?language=printer, accessed June 17, 2011.

Schor, Juliet. 1998. *The Overspent American: Why We Want What We Don't Need.* New York: HarperPerrenial.

Schor, Juliet. 2010. "Morality and Critique in Consumer Studies." *Journal of Consumer Culture* 10: 274–280.

Schor, Juliet. 2010. *Plenitude: The New Economics of True Wealth.* New York: Penguin. (Paperback title, *True Wealth*)

Schor, Juliet, and Margaret Willis. 2009. "Does Changing a Light Bulb Lead to Changing the World? Civic Engagement and the Ecologically Conscious Consumer." Unpublished draft of paper presented at the 2011 Consumer Culture and Civic Participation conference, Madison, WI, March 4.

Schwartz, Barry. 2004. *The Paradox of Choice: Why More Is Less.* New York: HarperCollins.

"Scientists Work to Develop Environmentally Friendly Bombs." 2008. *Fox News*, May 28. http://www.foxnews.com/story/0,2933, 358701,00.html, accessed January 20, 2012.

Shaw, Deirdre, and Terry Newholm. 2002. "Voluntary Simplicity and the Ethics of Consumption." *Psychology and Marketing* 19(2): 167–185.

Shell, Ellen Ruppell. 2009. *Cheap: The High Cost of Discount Culture*. New York: Penguin Books.

Sherman, Rachel. 2005. "Producing the Superior Self: Strategic Comparison and Symbolic Boundaries among Luxury Hotel Workers." *Ethnography* 6(2): 131–158.

Sherry, John. 1983. "Gift Giving in Anthropological Perspective." *Journal of Consumer Research* 10: 157–168.

Simon, Bryant. 2009. *Everything but the Coffee: Learning about America from Starbucks*. Berkeley: University of California Press.

Simon, Bryant. 2010. "The Rough Democracy of Buying." http://redroom.com/member/bryant-simon/blog/the-rough-democracy-of-buying, accessed January 10, 2012.

Simon, Bryant. 2011. "Not Going to Starbucks: Boycotts and the Out-Sourcing of Politics in the Branded World." *Journal of Consumer Culture* 11(2): 145–167.

Simpson, Charles, and Anita Rapone. 2000. "Community Development from the Ground Up: Social Justice Coffee." *Human Ecology Review* 7(1): 46–57.

Slater, Don. 2010. "The Moral Seriousness of Consumption." *Journal of Consumer Culture* 10: 280–284.

Smith, Jackie, and Hank Johnston. 2002. *Globalization and Resistance: Transnational Dimensions of Social Movements*. Lanham, MD: Rowman and Littlefield.

Smith, Julia. 2010. "Fair Trade and the Specialty Coffee Market: Growing Alliances, Shifting Rivalries." In *Fair Trade and Social Justice: Global Ethnographies*, ed. Sarah Lyon and Mark Moberg. New York: New York University Press.

Solidarity eXchange. 2011. "Transfair USA Name Changed to Fair Trade USA: Where Is the Movement?" June 13. http://solidarityexchange.com/node/ 5931, accessed January 18, 2012.

"Special Report: Voting with Your Trolley—Food Politics." 2006. *Economist* 381(8507) (December 9): 81.

Szasz, Andrew. 2007. *Shopping Our Way to Safety: How We Changed from Protecting Our Environment to Protecting Ourselves*. Minneapolis: University of Minnesota Press.

Talbot, John. 2004. Grounds for Agreement: The Political Economy of the Coffee Commodity Chain. Lanham, MD: Rowman and Littlefield.

Tarmann, Kevin. 2002. *The Fair Trade Coffee Movement: Norm Change or Niche Marketing?* PhD dissertation, University of Virginia.

Taussig, Doron. 2006. "Bite the Hand." *Philadelphia City Paper*, June 15, 22–27.

Taylor, Alex, III. 2006. "Toyota: The Birth of the Prius." *CNN Money*. http://money.cnn.com/2006/02/17/news/companies/mostadmired_fortune_toyota/index.htm, accessed June 17, 2011.

Ten Thousand Villages. 2010. "Annual Report." http://www.tenthousandvillages.com/php/about.us/index.php#annual_report, accessed January 30, 2012.

TransFair USA. 2010. "Impact Report: Fair Trade Certified Coffee." Oakland, CA. http://www.transfairusa.org/sites/ default/files/Coffee_Impact_ Report_1.pdf, accessed June 23, 2011.

Tucker, Robert C., ed. 1972. *The Marx-Engels Reader*. New York: Norton.

Tuckman, Jo. 2001. "Left behind in Mexico, Family Members Mourn Migrants Who Died in Arizona." Associated Press, May 28.

United Students for Fair Trade. 2011. "United Students for Fair Trade Withdraws Support from Fair Trade USA/Transfair—Calls for Reform to Fair Trade Standards." Press release, October 25. http://usft.org/node/373, accessed January 17, 2012.

Veblen, Thorstein. [1899] 1953. *The Theory of the Leisure Class*. New York: Mentor.

Walker, Rob. 2008. *Buying In: The Secret Dialogue between What We Buy and Who We Are*. New York: Random House.

Wansink, Brian. 2006. *Mindless Eating: Why We Eat More Than We Think*. New York: Random House.

Weissman, Michaele. 2008. *God in a Cup: The Obsessive Quest for the Perfect Coffee*. Hoboken, NJ: Wiley.

Wherry, Frederick. 2006. "The Social Sources of Authenticity in Global Handicraft Markets: Evidence from Northern Thailand." *Journal of Consumer Culture* 6(1): 5–32.

Wherry, Frederick. 2008. *Global Markets and Local Crafts: Thailand and Costa Rica Compared*. Baltimore: Johns Hopkins University Press.

White, Harrison. 2002. *Markets from Networks: Socioeconomic Models of Production*. Princeton, NJ: Princeton University Press.

Williams, Alex. 2007. "Buying into the Green Movement." *New York Times*, July 1.

Wuthnow, Robert. 1996. *Poor Richard's Principle*. Princeton, NJ: Princeton University Press.

Zavestoski, Stephen. 2002. "The Social-Psychological Bases of Anticonsumption Attitudes." *Psychology and Marketing* 19(2): 149–165.

Zelizer, Viviana. 1997. *The Social Meaning of Money*. Princeton, NJ: Princeton University Press.

Zinn, Howard. 2004. "The Optimism of Uncertainty." *CommonDreams.org*. November 8. http://www.commondreams.org/views04/1108-21.htm, accessed August 9, 2012.

Zukin, Sharon. 2004. *Point of Purchase: How Shopping Changed America*. New York: Routledge.

INDEX

Page numbers in italics refer to illustrations.

ABOUT THE AUTHOR

Keith R. Brown is Assistant Professor of Sociology at Saint Joseph's University.